MY LIFE

With(out)

RANCH

A Rollercoaster Journey to Self-Worth

BY HEATHER WYATT

For permission requests, write to the publisher, addressed "Attention: Permissions Coordinator," at editor@5050press.com

ISBN-13: 9781947048195

Library of Congress Control Number
LCCN:
Edited by: Megan Cassidy-Hall

This is a work of creative nonfiction. The events are portrayed to the best of the author's memory. While all the stories in this book are true, some names and identifying details have been changed to protect the privacy of the people involved.

Printed in the U.S.A. First Edition, September, 2018

For David Earp, and all the others
I love more than my luggage.

List of Recipes

Introduction

Christopher Robinson, as he will be referred to in this story, was wearing a red and white gingham shirt. The shirt had buttons (in which every button was buttoned, including the top one on the collar) and long sleeves. He had a sandy-blonde bowl cut, bright, blue eyes, and lips the color of a strawberry-flavored Blow Pop. Imagine Kevin from *Home Alone* before his parents left him in that attic.

It was time for recess. At that time, the playground situation at White Oak Elementary School in Chattanooga, Tennessee included a broad expanse of swing sets, slides, monkey bars and the other traditional accouterment usually included in a playground setting. Beyond that area, which was complete with dark brown wood chips and dirt, was a giant grassy field.

The playground itself was limited to the standard activity of playing. It's where I barely sprained my wrist one day. It's where I hung upside down from the camel-colored metal bar. It's where I tried, and failed, to use my arm strength to go across the monkey bars. It's where I tied my LA Gear shoes and played with Monica and Brandie.

Leaving the confines of the playground meant that you were running off into the field with your friends. It's here that the seedlings of gossip were planted. This is where children learned to be assholes. It's where the bullying took place because teachers were too concerned with injuries on the playground to pay attention to the small groups of children talking in circles in the grass.

One day, in a cluster of my friends, Christopher Robinson, resident brat and bully, came charging toward us. He said some classic mean line I can't remember. If I had to guess, he called one of us dumb because I remember that my response was, "No, *you're* dumb." I hadn't quite mastered my "diss" skills yet.

All I know is that right after my retort, Christopher Robinson screamed, "You're fat!" And then he punched me in the stomach. Mortified, I tried to play it off. Nobody did anything other than laugh or feel pity. I didn't tattle because "snitches get stitches" and all that. I can still feel the blow to my belly. It wasn't too hard. We were only five or six years old. But somehow, I can feel the breath catch in my lungs. It was shock mostly. I had never considered fatness before.

That was the first moment I felt ashamed of my body.

Photos of me as a child show an average looking kid with round cheeks. However, at an early age, I became aware that even though I was about as "normal" as any other red-blooded American girl, I wasn't skinny. I was also aware that this was bad.

Soon after my encounter with Christopher Robinson on the playground, I stumbled upon another moment that proved people were monitoring my size.

During the summers as a child in Chattanooga, I spent my time at my Grandma's house. She was a full-time babysitter to other kids, so I went there every day with my cousins, Mark and John, while my parents were at work. My memories of my Grandma's house as a child are as vivid (if not more) than any other memories that I have. The driveway was gravel and had a drop off on the side. My family calls it "the wall." "The wall" is just a foot-tall line of stone that could easily be miscalculated. I'm still terrified I'm going to drive off the edge of the wall every time I go to her house.

In those days, my Grandma didn't have vinyl siding, but the porch looked about the same as it does now. The steps leading up to the porch are uneven. One of the steps is about a foot tall and the others are half that size. Inside, the carpet was burgundy shag. The living room held dark brown furniture and my Grandma's piano. But the real hang-out spot was the den. It was where the giant box TV sat. We had to go up to the TV to change the channel. (Side note: their current TV still sits on top of that old TV and has for years.) It's where the toys were. It's where I played kitchen and Hot Wheels. It's where I watched *The Price is Right* and *Hee Haw* reruns with my Grandpa.

Much of my childhood was spent at my Grandma's. My grandmother grew up with eight brothers and sisters. Her parents died when she was only ten. She was raised by roughnecks on a farm in Roanoke, Virginia. She's often told me stories about the way some of them mistreated her. I know I'm not the only one with a grandma that feels it necessary to point out body weight, but my Grandma isn't often shy with her commentary. It started young.

One day, during the summer, she had made exactly six buttermilk biscuits. My cousin John, my cousin Mark, and I went into the kitchen to grab one. We ran back to the den to enjoy our breakfast. A few minutes later, the boys said they wanted a second biscuit, and I agreed.

3

We all ran back in to the kitchen to get one. Grandma had made six, so there should have been another one for each of us.

Mark and John asked her for a biscuit and she obliged. When I held out my hand for my seconds, she furrowed her brow and gave me a firm, "No."

When I protested her response, I provided the best logic I could muster. If they had a second biscuit, I could have one too. I've never been a math whiz, but even I could work that out. After she listened to me whine for a moment she just said, "Do you want to look like an elephant?"

It's funny what moments stick out to you from childhood. I can't remember every time someone made a comment about my weight, but when I think about this day, about my grandmother telling a perfectly healthy, normal child that having a second biscuit would make her look like an elephant, I remember every detail. I remember the way the sun was shining through the lace curtains. I remember the makeshift kitchen door (about two feet tall that stays closed with a latch) that hung between us. I remember my cousins standing about a foot away, sniggering.

My grandma has made a few jabs about my weight over the years, but that was most definitely the first. She longed for a thin, blonde-haired, blue-eyed girl as a granddaughter. If we're being honest, she really just wanted a boy. I think she loves me. I love her. And God knows someone else would have made me aware of my body and the reasons they feel that I should be ashamed of it at some point, but when I look back and try to find a root...the first seeds, the image of that scene so many years ago is always there, hanging like leftover biscuit dough from a rolling pin.

My body issues really blossomed in high school "Purple. And. White. Purple and White!" Holt High School in Tuscaloosa, Alabama used to be the armpit of the county school system. They are in the process of building a new school now, but when I went there, it was on its last legs. The building itself was old and run down. It stuck out like a sore thumb on what we used to call "River Road."

The football stadium, if you could call it that, had rocky concrete bleachers painted purple and white on one side to display Holt's emblem. We were the Holt Ironmen. Our colors, as you may have guessed, were purple and white. I don't mean the good purple, either. Purple is my favorite color, but I prefer more of a sophisticated eggplant color, not a knockoff of Barney the Dinosaur.

I had friends in high school, but I largely felt uncomfortable there. I was made fun of quite often for my weight, and even though I didn't get made fun of for much else, that was the only ammunition kids needed. I can think of a few culprits who tormented me, but none more than Chester Allen Arthur. No, that isn't his real name, but I'm protecting him here because, in full disclosure, he's apologized to me multiple times for his high school behavior.

Before he was a good human being, however, he made my teenage life a nightmare. Walking down the hall one day, purple lockers on either side of the wall, I heard what sounded like my name in the distance. It had the same number of syllables but wasn't an exact match, so I ignored it. The person who yelled the name said it again and then again. As the voice got closer, I could tell that it was Chester Allen Arthur, but I still knew he wasn't saying *my* name, so I kept walking, trying to ignore him.

Finally, it occurred to me that he was saying "Heifer Weigh-It." After a few attempts of him saying this name in my ear, I finally realized he'd made up a nickname for me. Clunky as this nickname was, I was hoping it didn't stick. Sure, it kind of sounded like my name, but it certainly wasn't an exact match, and it didn't really roll of the tongue.

My hopes that this nickname would disappear into the noise of the busy hallway, like last week's gossip about someone getting drunk or pregnant or having an abortion, fizzled quickly. It became a "thing." From then on, I heard that nickname nearly every day my last two years of high school. Every time that name would exit the mouth of people I now hope have constant diarrhea, my spine would tingle from the top of my back all the way down to my tailbone. My chest would burn, and torrents of hot red blood would fill my cheeks under my skin. My tear ducts would threaten to overflow, but I never let them. I could not let them see me cry.

Walking to computer science one day, I was about to enter the classroom when I heard my recently donned moniker. I ignored it and tried to rush into the room. Before I knew it, I felt a hand grasp my wrist so tightly I couldn't shake it loose. There he was, Chester Allen Arthur. A blonde-haired, blue-eyed boy with pale skin mixed with a strawberry-red hue. He was torturing me with a smile on his face that exuded innocence but was evil in reality.

With my wrist in his hand, despite my efforts to take it away, he flipped my hand over and then with his other hand, sprayed my arm with a can of compressed air. At first, it just felt like a cold rush of really concentrated wind hitting one spot on my arm. As he forced it to stay there, I started to feel the burn. Now that I know what getting a tattoo feels like, I can only liken the pain to that. It felt like tiny needles scraping one area of my arm. I was finally able to beg him to stop but by that point, everyone was laughing. I had a hive-looking wound on my arm, and there I was, trying once again to pretend I was fine.

So, even though I guess you could say this journey started in an official capacity in early 2009, this roller coaster ride began creeping up the first hill years ago. I spent most of my high school years at a pleasantly plump weight, and then in college, the terrible boyfriend/breakup cliché kicked in, and I ballooned into another category spurred on by an incessant need to eat a large meal after every class.

Then it became a real issue because diabetes runs in my family. I hated myself and who I was, and I couldn't sleep because of complications from my heartburn. Then, one day, early in 2009, something changed.

I looked at the clock. 3:37AM. I felt a gurgle in my throat and a fiery swirl in my chest. While on my back and side, my breasts came together near my neck, making it difficult to breathe. I rolled over to my belly. I took a long body pillow, placed it vertically under my stomach beginning at my neck and ending in the center of my thighs. I propped my head up on a couple pillows and with my arms stretched at each side. I finally fell asleep in a face down position.

Three hours later, my alarm went off. I knew that the issue I was having with sleeping came from complications of severe acid reflux. I've always been a bit of an expert in diagnosing myself with mental and physical ailments. The diagnosis of heartburn, though, was an easy one to come to as I noticed that every time I ate, I nearly regurgitated the contents later when it erupted from my esophagus into my mouth.

As I got ready for work, I groggily stumbled to the bathroom and like every morning, I did my best to avoid the glance of my naked body in the mirror. It's weird because sometimes I obsessively stare at myself in the mirror. I can be caught looking in mirrors at restaurants, or in car rearview mirrors for minutes at a time. There are other times, however, that I can't bring myself to see what I look like.

This day was typical for the most part, but because my hypothyroidism requires a bi-annual doctor's visit, I couldn't just go to work and come home like normal; I had a checkup that afternoon. My thyroid is lazy. In fact, my doctor once said, "it looks like your thyroid essentially does nothing." Sure, saying you have a bad thyroid is pretty much the equivalent of "I have big bones" to many people, but believe me when I tell you, it's real. And as I get older, it gets harder and harder to function every day.

So, I go a couple times a year to have my blood tested so they can tell me that nothing has changed and refill my prescriptions. This day, in 2009, it was time for an appointment that I had been putting off for quite a while. I hated going. I was no fool. I knew that patients couldn't get to their exam room without going through the lake of fire that included ear thermometers, blood pressure cuffs, and worst of all, the scale.

The thought of getting on a scale at the doctor's office is one that strikes fear in the hearts of millions of people everywhere. It's such a real fear that there's even a name for it: gravitophobia. When you throw this term in the search bar, the definition states that this fear of the scale is irrational, but I disagree.

Not only do insurance companies provide a number they derive from scientific "facts" stating what they feel people *should* weigh according to sex and height, but society also gives out a different (usually lower) number they believe is acceptable.

I don't know what a person should weigh, but I feel confident that at no point in my entire life have I ever remotely been close to what I'm *supposed* to weigh. The day I finally sucked it up and went to the doctor, I was miles away, more than double what the number *should* be.

The door creaked open to the waiting room. I signed in and took a seat. To my left was a man with a mesh, camouflage hat. His flannel shirt was tucked into high-waisted jeans that were being held up by suspenders. He was at least 600 years old. He was having a political conversation loudly with another elderly gentleman across the way. It was clear I wouldn't agree with much he said, so I tried not to listen. This wasn't new for the South or this waiting room. I somehow managed to find a primary physician who also happens to be the doctor for every card-carrying member of AARP in Tuscaloosa County.

I was called to pay a co-pay and then instructed to sit down. I waited around 30 minutes before I was called back. Somewhere between the time I left my seat and the moment I was guided back to the holding area where they keep the rest of the cattle, I made a defiant decision *not* to weigh that day. This wasn't a fascist regime and I wasn't a prisoner of war. I was an overweight human who didn't have to fucking weigh if she didn't want to.

I walked with my head held high.

"I'm not weighing today." I said. *Yeah, take that, asshole.*

"Please step on the scale, ma'am."

So, I stepped on the scale because I'm all talk, but I closed my eyes and asked in an apologetic tone, "Please do not tell me what the number is."

She obliged this request and led me to the exam room where I promptly sat on the plasticy leather exam chair and the crunchy paper they use to separate our pants germs from the rest of the population. Then, I waited.

9

A map of the world was on the wall to the left.

Hmmm. I didn't know that is where Bulgaria is. Why do I think everything is in South America?

I took a glance at the tongue depressors and before a wave of anxiety could engulf me completely, thinking about the wooden stick diving down my throat in search for strep as a child, the doctor walked in.

He shook my hand.

"Hi. How are you?" he said pleasantly as if I didn't know that he did a quick read through of my chart before he came in.

"Oh, I'm just fine." I found Bulgaria on the map again, so I didn't have to look him in the eyes.

"The nurse told me that you didn't want to see your weight. Is that true?"

I don't remember the thoughts I had in the three seconds that followed that question, but I do remember what happened *after* those three seconds.

I began crying in the doctor's office. It wasn't really a sob. It was more like I was talking in a Diane Sawyer interview in which I'm going over my awful experience and tell her I'm trying not to cry, and then she hands me a tissue because I'm clearly about to start crying. I'm not sure exactly what came over me. I think it was a culmination of the insecurities I have about my weight, worrying about my health, and hating my body. Perhaps I had waited too long to address those issues.

"Do you cry a lot?" Suddenly, it felt like he was my therapist, and I needed a sofa to lie on.

The truth was, I didn't cry a lot. I don't think there's anything wrong with crying, and I do my fair share of it when I'm listening to an 80's hair band love ballad because sometimes a girl needs a good cry but for the most part, I shut down the part of my brain that feels the feelings I don't particularly like.

The doctor told me that I needed to start exercising and eating better. He suggested I join Weight Watchers. The most striking thing he said to me though was, "If you don't do something about this now, you will be diabetic by the time you turn 30." At this time, I was 25 years old. My mother is diabetic, and I know the struggles she had and continues to go through to make sure her blood sugar is normal. I didn't want to have something like that. Especially if it was my own fault.

Thus my "journey" began. I started blogging and lost weight with a fury from 2009 until 2012. I was down 115 pounds in April of 2012, almost exactly 3 years after I started. In some ways, I went slow. I had discovered this brilliant balance of fun and food. Then, things got way harder. My thyroid slowed my metabolism down, my fervor for dieting was fleeting and I was knocking on the door of my 30th year.

No matter what I did, I couldn't lose any more weight. I found this to be devastating considering that I hadn't reached my goal weight and all joy from the initial 115 pounds evaporated and I judged myself solely on the fact that I was no longer losing weight. I was a failure. Over the next two years, I gained 10 pounds. Looking back on that now, I wish I hadn't been so upset about that. For some reason though, I couldn't get past the fact that I was somehow gaining weight despite my best efforts to exercise hard and eat healthy most of the time.

It was also during that time that I met the world's best boyfriend. Sure, he has flaws but for me, he's perfect. The only problem with perfect is that he's all, "I don't care what you weigh. Let's eat, drink and be merry together." So, I went from only putting on 10 pounds to putting on about 60.

This little hiccup has given my mental health a run for its money. On the one hand, I'm still nowhere near where I was when I first started. I don't just mean that in terms of numbers. I don't just eat what I want when I want. I exercise nearly every day, and I am always mindful of what I'm eating. That's a positive thing. What is particularly trying is that even at 75-80% effort, I'm not maintaining, I'm gaining at a steady rate. I don't want pity, but you have to admit it would be pretty frustrating to be conscious of your intake and activity level 100% of the time and still get a bigger number on the scale every week.

One thing that I struggle with is that since I've started the blog, many people have told me that I've inspired them. This makes me uncomfortable because I still struggle with considering myself a failure. The things I've accomplished in my education and career mean nothing to me because I never reached my goal weight and I've put on extra pounds. I'm working on that, and it's not always easy.

What I have realized is that I'm not the only one aboard this struggle bus. So often we see cookbooks and diet narratives that show the success of the finished product. I was scared to write about food because I didn't feel as if I earned it. Then I decided that was silly. I have a lifetime of experience eating and I have at least seven years' experience learning to treat my body better.

I want this book to show you and myself that we are never finished, that it's OK to eat what we want sometimes. There are fun ways to eat healthier when we choose to do so, and that even though we may not be finished yet, we are perfect just the way we are.

I've learned these things by experience that manifests itself in essays that aren't always about food. In fact, I'm so convinced that what we eat is half the battle. The battle we have with ourselves, in our minds, has to be addressed before we can be happy and healthy.

Sure, I have some bits of advice (and recipes) but I'm also here to tell you that this ain't your typical before-and-after photo shoot. This is a book that says, "I'm with you. This life thing is hard. Here are the problems we should work on to stop hating ourselves."

1

Quick Fixes Have Never and Will Never Work

The first time I remember actively trying to lose weight was in high school. I had had just about enough of the nickname, "Heifer Weigh-it" and wanted to be skinny like everyone else. Looking back at photos, I'd take my high school body in a second, but back then, I felt like a giant scraping the lockers on both sides of the halls as I walked. Despite that, I still felt invisible. I was in the beginning stages of feeling unworthy because of my body.

Being impatient my entire life, my newfound quest to lose weight was going to need to be a quick one. I remembered seeing an ad for Richard Simmons' FoodMover. It was a plastic, wallet-sized food tracker containing windows with images of the types of foods I could have per day. So, there were eight windows for water, a few for fats, carbs, proteins, etc. When I consumed a serving of those items, I closed the corresponding window.

It was pretty simple, and judging by the before and after photos in the commercials, there was no way I wasn't going to be skinny within a couple weeks. I begged my parents to help me make this purchase and, in an effort to be supportive, they did. When it arrived, I tore open the plastic wrapping on the outside of the FoodMover and began flipping the pages of the guide that was included.

It was time for me to make my first Richard Simmons' approved lunch! As I began to analyze what I could and couldn't have, I realized that the diet was going to prove to be more difficult than I thought. I was preparing a salad but the salads that I had grown accustomed to, ones with luscious ranch dressing, bacon bits and crackers or croutons, were now off the table.

So, I prepared a salad that would make Richard Simmons proud and still allow me enough open windows on the FoodMover to have dinner that night. I looked at my plate and saw a quarter of a can of tuna, cucumbers, lettuce, and onions. No dressing. No cheese. No fun. *What the hell is this?* I thought to myself. I shook it off though. I ate that entire salad, pretending that the tuna I was eating was mixed with mayonnaise and that the lettuce and cucumbers were the bread, cheese, and Cool Ranch Doritos I so desired.

I don't really know how long I was on the Richard Simmons diet, but I must have given up quickly because that salad is the only starvation-y meal I remember having in high school.

Fast forward a few years to college when I decided that I needed to try every breakfast and lunch menu item out in the city of Tuscaloosa each day for 2 straight years. A tumultuous relationship followed by a depression-inducing breakup from that relationship, didn't make for the best diet plan.

Sadly, I've never been the kind of person who loses her appetite when I'm having relationship trouble. It's quite the opposite. I'm all: breakfast, snack, lunch, snack, second lunch, snack, dinner, dessert, snack, snack, drink-until-drunk, snack.

I'd venture to say that I gained roughly 75-100 pounds as I rounded out my college career. As the romantic relationship came crashing down, my mind was a cluster of self-doubt and self-esteem issues. When it ended, I convinced myself the only way I could be happy was if I lost weight.

Since I hadn't learned my lesson in high school, I decided to try yet another quick fix. This time, it was with the Atkins diet. Now, to give the Atkins diet credit, I never followed it by the book. I didn't do any induction phases or recommended meals. Essentially, I cut out all carbs.

At first, I was living the high life. I survived on mostly steak, bacon and eggs, and salads made with the same three proteins. I'd throw in some grilled chicken and vegetables occasionally when I felt like being fancy, but for the most part, I had a high-fat, high-sodium diet to go with my low carb ways.

It worked like a charm in the beginning. I dropped 40 pounds in a couple months. Then, I remembered what bread tasted like. I began to sneak carbs in secret. I would have a piece of bread here, a skosh of potato there, and an "Oh, do you mind if I have just one bite of your pasta?"

As I came back down to earth and realized that I was missing out on a whole world of starchy goodness, I became a monster. Deprivation didn't suit me well. When I was avoiding carbs, I was mean. When I was eating them, I was eating *all* of them. It was ugly.

3

The advantage of a low-carb diet is rapid weight loss, but I found way more disadvantages to a diet that cuts out carbs completely. So, if you are considering a low or no carb diet, there are some things you should know, based on my experience and level of will power.

First, you will inevitably crave and/or eat bread and pasta again. When you do, your body will absorb them at a faster rate because it has grown used to not having them.

Second, a low carb diet often has you craving more high fat, high sodium foods like the bacon and steak I mentioned earlier to make up for what you're missing. Believe it or not, you should not be eating a rib-eye steak and a jar of peanut butter for dinner every night.

Lastly, it is flat out *not* a sustainable diet (or it wasn't for me). If you want to lose a couple pounds for a specific event, you could drop carbs for a few weeks. But just be warned that when you start eating them again, the weight will come back on far more quickly than it came off.

Once I stopped living the no-carb lie, I came back to my former eating habits full throttle. I gained every bit of the 40 pounds back and then doubled that. My mental status and the number on the scale brought me to an all-time low and then in 2009, an unexpected fire set ablaze inside me and I was ready to make a change. To this day, I still don't know if there was an exact moment I decided I was ready to embark on a multi-year journey to lose weight or if it was a culmination of things, but I did a complete 180.

I will talk about exercise later, but in terms of food, I joined Weight Watchers as the doctor recommended. For the first time in my life, I was breaking down my weight goals into smaller chunks.

I've said, "I need to lose 100 pounds" to myself many times in the past. In fact, as I type this, I'm sitting here thinking I would be happy if I lost another 40-50 pounds. The problem with this mentality is that it is a perfect setup for failure. If you decide you want to be a surgeon at the age of 18, you don't begin that process by cutting open your Dad's belly on the kitchen table and try to remove his appendix when it bursts. You have to go to college, then med school, then you have to be a cast member on *Grey's Anatomy,* and you'll probably end up dying in a plane crash anyway.

The point is, wouldn't it be nice if instead of saying, "I need to lose half my body weight before I can exist as a human being," why don't you say, "I'd like to begin eating better today." If you're a numbers person, focus on losing five pounds before you lose fifty.

Accomplishing small goals keeps you motivated. Self-motivation is the *only* way to achieve success in the numbers game. The goal of this book is ultimately to say that staying healthy is a daily struggle. You need to worry more about loving who you are right now, but that doesn't mean you aren't allowed to try to lose weight if that would make you happier and healthier.

Here are my two most important tips:

1) Start slow.
2) Don't let the number on the scale dictate your mood or direction.

As someone who is incredibly Type A, Weight Watchers was the most suitable option for me in terms of diet plans. It incorporated my weight and activity level to determine how many "points" I would be allowed in a day. Since I'm an avid user of a planner, tracking what I ate during the day wasn't a problem. Also,

Weight Watchers took into account how many grams of fiber, protein, carbohydrates, etc. were included in each food.

The best part was, I started off slow. I was still eating quite a bit of food each day. As the weight came off, so did the point allowance. Most diets shock your body, which means quick weight loss at first without learning the most important lesson: maintaining. Weight Watchers understands this and therefore it's a slower, but more effective process than most weight loss programs.

I was diligent on Weight Watchers for around three years and was quite successful. As expected, my weight did come off more quickly in the beginning. It took me around 6 months to lose 50 pounds. Then I plateaued dramatically. The next 65 pounds took around 2 and a half years. As I mentioned earlier, by April of 2012, I was down 115 pounds.

While this was a tremendous accomplishment, I still didn't see myself as a finished product. My self-image improved over years past. However, looking at myself naked still felt like a chore. I'd peer at the extra skin on my arms, lament at my belly undercarriage that still hung low, resting just above my vagina. I saw the cellulite in my thighs, the roundness of my hips. I would try on my roommate's clothes and see that even after losing 115 pounds, I still couldn't come close to fitting in her shirts or pants.

On top of the low self-esteem, I found the whole process exhausting. I had been doing it for three years and didn't see an end in sight. I couldn't accept that maybe, just maybe, I should have been OK with who I was: a healthy, average-sized woman who had a list of other accomplishments that had nothing to do with weight.

Since April of 2012, I have gained back around 60 of those pounds. It hasn't been a proportionate weight gain. Being the type

A person that I am, I have recorded a weekly weight since I began in 2009. There have been periods of not weighing, especially when I'm feeling particularly bad about myself, but I have an idea of what the number on the scale has been every week for around 8 years.

From 2012-2014, I felt a decline in motivation, yet I never stopped counting points, and I never stopped exercising and "starting over" to "get serious" each week. During that period, while the flame was dwindling, I felt crushing disappointment every time I got on the scale and realized that I wasn't losing weight anymore. I felt resentful that I was still denying myself many drinks and foods, and going hard at the gym, only to find that it was no longer working. In my head, this "journey" started manifesting itself into a giant, two-headed, lumpy, green beast that I was pushing against and trying to defeat but that wouldn't leave me alone.

I'd never even given myself a chance to hold up a trophy and already, I was declaring myself a loser. The fear of returning to my 2009 weight was all-powerful. The old weight seemed imminent, and it clouded my judgment. In the midst of this mental turmoil, I didn't realize that I had only gained 10 pounds of the 115 pounds in 2 years. I couldn't see that the reality of the situation was nothing more than a plateau, and that while it was frustrating, it wasn't that big of a fucking deal. I wish I could go back to 2014, hurl a bucket of ice water in my face, and say, "WHAT IS WRONG WITH YOU?!"

My will to lose weight was so strong at first that I couldn't see anything else around me. I didn't consider (and still don't much of the time) that I'm a human being, regardless of the number on the scale. There is an impenetrable fear associated with numbers and dieting that creates obsessive thoughts. We view success as weight loss and failure as weight gain. It's a dangerous, psychological game that we play with ourselves.

Because now, I'd give anything to go back to my 2014 weight, knowing I'd only put on 10 pounds instead of 60 or 70. Now, I feel exposed. Social media and a blog in which I discuss this journey every week proves that at one time, I wasn't a loser who couldn't keep the weight off. I was someone worth admiring.

That's the other issue. Back in the day, after losing 115 pounds, people called me an inspiration. The first few times someone said that to me, I was shocked. I mean, I was still just a chubby girl who didn't think what she had done was any big deal and "I still have such a long way to go but thank you."

I couldn't be an inspiration. It was too much pressure. And yet, multiple people told me that. A woman from work was so inspired by my weight loss, she went and lost more weight than I did. Suddenly, motivation was contagious around the office and just as everyone else was getting started, I was the aging, poorly made car who had just hit the 100,000-mile mark.

Fast forward a few years later when I finally decided to get some therapy. I used the discount therapy my school offered, which meant my therapist was a grad student. I didn't mind. She had a supervisor and I felt it was worth a shot. The thing that I didn't 100% love was that she was a bit too "by the book." Oh, and I think she was always aiming to see me cry. I didn't often give her the satisfaction.

Our first several meetings were spent talking about weight. She could see it was my darling, my obsession, a monster at the center of all my obsessive thoughts. We were trying to get at the root of the issue.

Suddenly, it occurred to me that the reason I was so anxious and depressed about weight had less to do with the numbers and more to do with the fact that I felt like I was a failure, a fraud, someone unworthy to talk about weight or health. My mind kept returning to a broken record of thoughts. *I am not an inspiration; I'm a letdown, a botched attempt at success that went horribly wrong.* The other details of my life were floating in bubbles aimlessly around me and with each negative thought, they were popping, leaving a tiny ring of soap on the ground.

Nothing seemed to matter. All that mattered is that I put myself out there and failed, proving that once again, I couldn't finish something I started. This connection I have to weight can be applied to every aspect of my life: my relationships, my writing, my teaching, my confidence. With every swirling, self-lamenting, shame filled thought I have, I'm taking a blowtorch to a life that could be happy, fulfilling, and meaningful.

So, let's stop doing that maybe? Because of the rut, I went back to my old ways by experimenting again with low carb, using fitness apps, and counting calories. I tried doing nothing. I tried planning everything. I searched for a "quick fix" again even though I knew good and damn well it doesn't exist.

My goal now is to find a balance of health and happiness. I have a family history of high blood pressure and diabetes. Some of those symptoms appear when I've been eating or drinking too much. My health is important to me, and I want to re-direct my focus to one that includes a healthy (mental and physical) lifestyle.

I always want to have a renewed faith that I will no longer associate numbers with "success" and "failure" and "good" and "bad." That will be the most challenging part because with most diet programs, the weigh-in portion is what says thumbs up or thumbs down. I have to remember that when I started in 2009, I was 25 years old. I'm now 33. I have an inactive thyroid and the activities I used to do as a 25-year-old don't come quite as easy now and that's OK.

Finally, I need to know that I'm capable of anything. And you are too. If I find myself getting trapped in the same mentalities, I need to re-focus again because I have to find something that provides a balance between achieving the health goals I have for myself while also remaining the person I am: a woman who enjoys her food and drink.

There are no quick fixes when it comes to weight. Body issues have a root. A seed was planted at some point and then it grew inside my brain, wrapping around it like kudzu in the South.

That means that the "fixing" isn't always about the scale. There are multiple facets to work on, including mental health. Truth be told, it's probably the most important part of the journey. If we can chip away at some of the damage we've inflicted upon ourselves over the years, physical and mental health will become a natural progression rather than an uphill battle. This is something I'm dealing with.

I wish there was a pill that turned our pumpkins into carriages, that we were suddenly the exact size we needed to have the perfect amount of confidence needed to survive in this body image obsessed world, but there's not. The act of being healthy mentally and physically and actually feeling that way too is an arduous process that never ends. I've been doing this shit my whole life, and it's horrific. I know that's about the worst pep talk ever but it's the truth. The bottom line is there will always be choices to make when it comes to both food and thoughts. Sometimes you will make better choices and sometimes you won't.

The first step is to have a mantra that consists of some type of positive assertion. "I am OK right now at this weight. I am a human being that deserves to be loved by myself and others no matter what I look like." If you believe that, or if you work to believe that, you may find your fitness and diet goals changing.

If you still want to change the numbers, start with small goals and work from there. If you're an inactive smoker whose diet has consisted of pizza and cigarettes for seven years and you want to get your life right, don't try to quit smoking cold turkey, eat only lettuce and run a mile in a week. See what I'm getting at? Let's be better in our minds and bodies together, at a normal pace.

Quick Fix Comfort Food Alternatives

Homemade Low-Cal Ranch

Ingredients:

- 3 ½ cups buttermilk
- 1 cup light mayonnaise (I'm very particular about mayonnaise. I don't use "salad dressing" mayo. Light is fine, but it has to be real!)
- 2 one-ounce packets of your favorite ranch dressing or seasoning mix
- 1 tablespoon garlic powder (If you don't like strong garlic flavor, leave this out or lessen it)
- 1 tablespoon onion powder

Note: If you're making this just for yourself and not a group, feel free to cut the recipe in half. This makes a huge batch!

Directions:

Plop the mayonnaise in a big bowl. Pour in the buttermilk half a cup at a time. This is an instance in which it's important not to throw everything in a bowl at once because you'll end up with clumps of mayo.

Stir the buttermilk in slowly making sure each half-cup portion gets mixed in evenly. I highly recommend using a whisk for this.

Once the mayonnaise and buttermilk are combined and there aren't a ton of mayo clumps, stir in the dressing mix, garlic powder and onion powder. Pop a lid on the bowl or container, stick it in the fridge and let it cool a bit then it's all yours.

Pro Tips:

Keep some low fat blue cheese on deck and mix it in to the dressing for home made "healthier" blue cheese dressing. I know it's weird, but I actually bring a small container of this dressing to most places I go for dinner. You can have 3 tablespoons of this dressing for less than 60 calories.

If you don't like ranch or get sick of it, I've also used a number of other sauces as a lower calorie dressing over the years including barbecue sauce, peanut sauce, salsa, and Dijon mustard.

Mock Thai Nachos for One
(Unless you're in the sharing mood)

There's a joint called Avenue Pub in downtown Tuscaloosa, Alabama. If you're ever in the area, I insist you go. If you live in Tuscaloosa and you haven't been, I'm publicly shaming you right now. They have pub food that rises above your average bar fare. Their burgers are amazing, as is their selection of craft beer.

When I go there though, I usually get the Thai Nachos—a giant plate of fried, house-made, flaky, crunchy, flour tortilla chips. On top of those is premium shredded chicken, peanut sauce, spicy Sriracha, sesame seeds and green onions. Each bite has the perfect balance of heat, cheese and protein and the peanut sauce adds a sweet and salty flare. I eat these uncontrollably because they are so damn good.

Before I give you the mock version, it's important to note that nothing compares to them so I'm not pulling off any miracles, here. However, the less caloric home version is also tasty!

Ingredients:

- 2 burrito-sized flour tortillas
- 1 grilled chicken breast
- ½ cup low fat (part skim) shredded mozzarella cheese
- 2 tablespoons peanut sauce
- 1 tablespoon Sriracha
- 1 tablespoon toasted sesame seeds
- 1 chopped green onion
- Non-stick cooking spray

14

Directions:

Pre-heat your oven to 350 degrees. While it's heating, take the flour tortillas and cut them into eighths. Essentially, you're looking for chip-sized triangles.

Place them on a baking sheet that you've lined with foil and sprayed with non-stick cooking spray and pop them in the oven. This is a trial and error thing but usually 6-7 minutes is plenty. You want them to be crisp but be careful because they will burn in a split second.

While they are baking, shred or dice the chicken into small pieces and chop the green onion.

Get the tortilla chips out of the oven.

Spread the chicken over the top. Add the cheese, peanut sauce and Sriracha.

Let the nachos bake for 3-4 minutes until the cheese is melted. When they come out of the oven, top with sesame seeds and green onion.

Serve immediately.

Waffle Fry Sliders

Ingredients:

- 1 bag frozen waffle sweet potato fries (you can also use regular if you can't find the sweet potato, but the sweetness works well with the pork)
- 1 pound barbecue pork (store bought or homemade)
- 1 package Provolone cheese
- Chives for garnish

Directions:

Prepare both the pork and waffle fries according to their package directions.

Once the waffle fries are done, crisp and cool enough to touch and the pork is warmed through, you can begin to assemble. All you're doing is finding waffle fries that are similarly sized (basically, pick the good ones) and using them as mini buns. You are making tiny pork sandwiches.

Before adding the top fry, add a small piece of the provolone (you can cut each slice of cheese into fourths) and a few chives.

Then, that's it! You have an adorable, fun slider. Between you and me, dipping these babies in a dollop of ranch or sour cream makes them even yummier.

2

Drain the Swamp

The phrase "drain the swamp" dates back to the early 1900s. Since the 2016 presidential election, the term has been given its second 15 minutes of fame. Though the true meaning of the phrase may be lost in a haze of media and political frenzy, it does have some merit.

I'm not an expert in politics, so I won't talk about any of that, (you're welcome) but I do feel that the term "drain the swamp" can apply to the folks you choose to have around you.

Your choice of company can affect your mental health, which in turn can have an impact on your physical health. Stop accommodating people who contribute to the downfall of your self-worth.

Over the past couple decades, as the pace of society has increased to a "panicked state of needing instant gratification," people spend far too much time apologizing for who they are and not only hang out with people they dislike, but spend time with people who are also toxic. Why do we repeatedly surround ourselves with people who make us want to reach for the nearest nerve pill?

The need many of us have to not offend someone is a sickness and one that we should work actively to stop. Trust me when I tell you, that shit isn't easy. First, think of the person who sucks the soul from your body the most. Is it a coworker you must share an office with? Or, is it a close family member you can't walk away from? If so, that's a little trickier.

If you conclude this person isn't connected to you by blood or a paycheck, then ask yourself this next question: Would you be sad if you never saw this person again? No? Drop them like it's hot. Do it. It's the most liberating thing you'll ever do.

A few years back, I had this friend who I will call Fiona. Fiona approached me every few weeks to ask if I could go get coffee or eat lunch, so we could have a "talk." In our circle of friends, she was known as the person who needed to talk out problems she was having with her friends on a regular basis.

Generally, I would have no idea what I had done prior to these "talks" to upset her. I'd go to meet Fiona, and at the beginning, I always had a sense of anxiety, a need to make sure whatever I had done could be resolved. I would have my apology ready, my speech that would entail words like, "I would never hurt you on purpose" and "yes, I can see how that upset you."

Eventually, I grew tired of said "talks" and decided that I was no longer going to participate. She overreacted to every sentence and every action in our friendship.

When Fiona dated guys, either in our friend group or from somewhere else, she became obsessed with them. Then when they lost interest in the relationship, she would lose her shit and expect you to lose it right along with her.

The words I'm using may sound petty. In fact, they sound a lot like a stereotypical female relationship, but it would be easy to dismiss the situation as "catty." Fiona needed something I couldn't give her, and I eventually realized I would go insane trying to maintain a friendship that was always going to be on the rocks.

The way that I eventually cut her off was to quit cold turkey. To this day, I'm not sure if I went about it the best way, but it *did* work. I neglected to respond to her requests for another "talk" and "ghosted" her, as the kids would say. Occasionally I still see her, but I always manage to avoid her. I can't stand the awkwardness.

Other than the once or twice every two years that I run into Fiona, I'm reminded of my total liberation from "the talks" and a person who was not adding anything to my life but stress. To be honest, since this "friend" and I were not even that close, I am still surprised that I let it go on as long as I did.

There are circumstances when you need to cut people out that have been a part of you for much longer. I was on the debate team in high school and college. Say what you will about my nerdiness, but my participation on the debate team got me a full ride to college. My senior year, my debate partner and friend turned into my best friend. I'll call her Tabitha. She and I spent many hours on the phone, spending time together, and of course, getting in trouble together.

Essentially, we were family. She remembered everything. I once called her to see what grade my own brother was in. Tabitha had the best gossip, and though we were a little different, she was my support system. She was there during every year of my terrible relationship with a manipulative, garbage bag of a human, giving me advice, listening to me cry and telling me she was fed up with me for continuously going back to a dumpster fire of a person. Sometimes, the words Tabitha said hurt, but I let her say them because she knew me, and she knew I shouldn't be with him.

One night, on a long drive from a debate tournament in college, something changed. The whole team was in the van, and I don't recall the context of the conversation, but the two of us were discussing our friendship to the rest of the folks in the van. Suddenly, as she was talking about me, Tabitha got emotional and said, "When Heather feels pain, I feel pain."

It was one of the best friendships I've ever had, and I don't take that lightly. At some point though, the friendship we once knew, changed. Three things happened that caused a shift. First, Tabitha fell in love with and spent all her time with her new boyfriend. That was fine. I adore him. However, it did mean that we saw each other less.

Second, during one of the breakup stints I had with a terrible boyfriend, my wild side emerged, and I started partying and becoming friends with Tabitha's two roommates, which changed the dynamic. The three of them didn't always see eye to eye, and my friendship complicated things even further.

Third and possibly most significantly, I developed a friendship with Jordan, Tabitha's former boyfriend and best friend from high school. Jordan understands me better than any human on this earth. It was an instant connection once we reunited in college. She may not admit it, but I think that hurt her.

Years passed, and though our relationship had changed, we made an effort to keep it going. We still talked all the time. Then, Tabitha got married. I was the maid of honor. Everything was good until she moved three states away. I was so happy for Tabitha because I wanted the best for her new life. Of course, as usual when someone moves, you start to see each other less.

Without Tabitha in town, my life began to look different. I have always been the kind of person to adjust to my "new normal" rather than clinging to the past. In my mind, Tabitha was gone. As a result, I think I failed our friendship in many ways. We still spoke but I could have made time to go see her. I could have made more of an effort.

The day Tabitha called and told me she was pregnant was interesting because at that point in my life, a baby for me was horrifying, so I guess I thought she would feel the same way. She was happy, so I was happy for her. But, because she was so far away, I couldn't be there to throw her a shower or go to an appointment with her that her husband couldn't make. We were in completely different places in our lives.

My friend (or as she's known in some circles, my wife) Cassandra and I made it once to visit Tabitha and the baby in North Carolina. I had instant affection for her baby and thought that even though we may not always be as close as we once were, we would still always be friends.

After a couple years, Tabitha and her family moved back to Tuscaloosa. I remember being happy that they were coming back but worried about what our friendship would look like now that so much time had passed. I worked, partied, and repeated that cycle every day. Now, she was a *mom*! Could I step up and be Aunt Heather?

I thought I was nailing it. I bought her baby presents and visited and attended birthday parties. I liked every photo on social media and yes, we still talked on the phone. The thing was, our relationship felt forced and stale. I wasn't ready to let it go because it was important to me, but every time I was around her, Tabitha made snarky remarks about when I left. When I called, she had a tone of irritation and disgust. It was exhausting. I felt like nothing I could ever do would be enough to make her happy.

On top of that, Tabitha had mom friends, and her life looked completely different from mine. I am not saying one was better or worse, but it *was* different. I think we both wanted the other to meet more in the middle and neither of us was willing to budge.

The tension between us was growing, and then our mutual friend made a remark to me about the reason Tabitha was mad at me. She said I had made some comment on Facebook when she found out Tabitha was pregnant again, which infuriated her. I was at a loss. I looked back on social media for hours trying to trace any comment that could be offensive. All I saw were statements of excitement for her.

I decided to call her and see what the hell I could have said that was so bad she'd been holding a multi-year grudge. As soon as I brought it up, Tabitha was ready to fight it out. She couldn't remember the exact words that I said, but she felt that I didn't want to be a part of her life anymore and it was obvious that time spent with her and her family was forced. I always seemed like I had one foot out the door. I told Tabitha it was hard to spend time with her because it always felt like she was mad at me, and that I wished she had talked to me much sooner.

Tabitha wasn't prepared to back down. She said a list of hateful things and ended with, "I guess I would still piss on you if you were on fire." It was at that point I realized our friendship was over. I shed one tear and then felt a strange sense of relief. Maybe I had known for a while that our friendship had been over, but this was the closure I needed.

The next day Tabitha emailed me a half-assed apology in which she never actually apologized but just said that she felt sorry the situation had escalated. I emailed her back and said it was obvious she really truly felt sorry, but neither of us made any moves to reconcile.

That was at least four or five years ago. Since then, Tabitha and I have bumped into each other. We speak like robots or two people who used to sit on the same pew at church. We are both ghosts of our former selves. Our mutual friend has tried to get us to "work things out." Strangely, I don't know what there would be to work out.

I don't have hard feelings toward her. I feel we both let the friendship go. At this point, trying to get back to where we were in high school and college would be an exhausting effort that neither of us have time for. Instead, we stay friends on Facebook, congratulate each other on monumental events, and go on with our lives. I can't speak for Tabitha, but I think we are both better for this change. The relationship we were having was one that was wreaking havoc on our nerves and emotions. Instead of remaining bitter and having repeated failed efforts to renew a connection that no longer exists, we admitted that people grow and change, and let it go.

Just because removing someone from your life will be difficult doesn't mean you shouldn't do it. You are on this planet for a short time. Your friendships shouldn't be tearing you to shreds emotionally.

I am forever grateful for Tabitha's friendship, not only because when it was good (It was great!) but also because it taught me a lot about my flaws in a friendship. I can be selfish, and I know that. I may not always outwardly say it but I'm legit thinking about myself 99% of the time. That's not to say I'm not there for people, but as a control freak, I don't adapt well to sudden change. My daily planner has a strict outline of the day's activities, which is why my former friend always felt like she was simply being "penciled in."

I also learned that the boyfriend who destroyed my self-esteem for 5 ½ solid years contributed to my friendship flaws. It was an all-consuming relationship, which forced everything and everyone else to the side. My former friend was a victim of my inability to prioritize. I was young and stupid. I'm still not perfect, but in this new chapter in life without her as a best friend, I'm better because she *was* my best friend.

The other major swamp drain I made was with the ex-boyfriend that I believe I referred to as a "garbage bag" earlier. He's someone who I haven't dated in over a decade, and I'm always saying that I have no hard feelings for him, but when I compare him to a plastic receptacle for waste, I have difficulty believing that proclamation, and I'm sure other people do too.

At the ripe old age of 17, "Devin" was a 22-year-old member of the University of Alabama debate team pursued me. I was horrified at first because I wasn't the only underage teen he had decided to make his target. Devin actually had a short-lived physical relationship with a former debate partner of mine. I am making him sound like a predator, and I don't know if that is exactly fair. However, though he didn't do anything that could land him in jail, Devin's manipulative spirit was certainly that of a blood thirsty lion smacking his lips for his next prey.

It's been awhile since I've written about Devin, but since this book is for me too, I realize that letting go of the past is part of the journey to mental and physical health. My self-esteem has never been stellar, but this relationship squashed it deep into the red clay ground of my surrounding southern landscape.

If I'm honest with myself, I never found Devin attractive. He was smart and charming, sure, but I was never drawn to him physically. I suppose some of that developed later but my initial decision to give him a chance was based on the fact that I'd never had a real boyfriend and the high school boys weren't talking to the chubby debate nerd. Here I was, a naïve girl who had never done more than kiss a boy at yearbook camp and maybe snuck a drink or two from my parent's liquor cabinet. I was a classic case of a budding teen, trying to be way more badass I than actually was.

Nothing exciting had happened to me, and I was lonely. Now, a college guy was ready to show me what I already knew—that I was smarter than those high school hacks and he could see that in me. I don't think this now. I was an idiot for falling for him. Back then, I blindly accepted Devin offer to "hang out." He said I was his "fatal attraction." I guess that showed our age difference because at that time, I had no idea what the hell he was talking about

I didn't tell my family about this relationship at first because 1) Devin was 22 and I was 17. 2) Devin was half African-American and half Cuban. My extended family is from the mountains of Tennessee, and they don't have the most shining track record when it comes to acceptance of interracial relationships. They are the extreme in the family, but some of their let's say "hesitations" of other races made me wary of telling people about them. In contrast, my parents raised me to love everyone. The slur-slinging Southern families you may see on in the media are *not* our kind of people.

25

When I finally told my parents, they most definitely weren't happy about the age difference, but said it was fine as long as school was always my priority.

Ultimately, neither his age, nor his race had anything do with the fact that he was just a scumbag.

His first misstep was breaking up with me after about six months. He did it on the river walk in town, and then asked me for a ride to church. Instead of telling him to walk, I did it. I drove the guy who had just broken my heart to church as if this was acceptable behavior. This was on a Friday. On a Monday, he wanted to get back together. I later found out a former fling of his was in town. In his mind, he was doing the right thing by calling it off, so he could "legally" cheat.

Of course, I took Devin right back, no questions asked. That's what dumb teen girls do. He flirted constantly with other women and made it clear that it was something I would just need to get over.

When we met, neither of us was religious. We went to protests, actively spoke against the strict religious laws of the South, and certainly didn't abide by any Christian rules. Then, out of nowhere, he got "saved."

Devin's friend started going to an Assembly of God church where they shout, sing, and speak in tongues. He convinced Devin to come and let the Lord wash away his sins, and Devin accepted. Then, it looked like I was next in line.

I remember walking into the shotgun church that was essentially a doublewide trailer. They took me in a small room and, without really explaining anything, asked me if I was ready to "accept Jesus in my heart." I looked at them both with a skeptical face. I wasn't ready that day. I grew up in church, but two men had just pulled me into a room and creepily asked if I was ready to give up funneling beer on the weekends. I wasn't there, y'all. I. Was. Not. There.

Eventually, they wore me down. Things were different between Devin and I ever since he got saved, so instead of telling him it wasn't going to work, I adapted and became a member of the Assembly of God church. It was weird at first, but I let it wash over me and suck me in. I was ready to sip the Kool-Aid if the time ever came. I started feeling convicted (their favorite term) every time I thought a curse word, wanted a drink, or questioned the Bible.

During that time, I befriended the resident Christian at my high school. She seemed like a perfect Christian, and then she met my boyfriend, and we all hung out a bit. I remember running to her on 9/11 thinking that the world was coming to an end, and she asked to pray with me.

I had completely converted my life for a boy. At some point, I became suspicious of the relationship Devin had with my perfect Christian friend. They hung out alone a couple times. Then, Devin started acting shady, and she kept bursting into tears every time I spoke to her. I asked my mom, and she told me Devin was cheating. I shrugged it off because I knew he wasn't my mom's favorite person.

One night, the hyper-Christian princess gave Devin a card and I asked to see it. He said no and claimed it was "private." Obviously, when he was gone, I opened it, and it had revealed they had kissed several times and that (gags) he was her first kiss.

I was beside myself. I called the girl to confirm, then hung up on her once she finally admitted it. It took me forever to track Devin down. I told him we were done. I ran to a friend's house. I cried and wanted to vomit.

The rest is kind of a haze. What I do know is that by that night, I had already decided to take him back. By then the trust was gone though, and I spent the next four years with someone who had cheated, and who I'm almost certain cheated again at some point.

During those years, I gained probably a hundred pounds. I found myself disgusting and would constantly complain about my weight and look to him to reassure me he wouldn't leave me. It's mortifying to be a prisoner to your own insecurities and also be someone's puppy, constantly begging your owner for attention.

I grew to love the church's young adult group, and I also loved singing on the praise team, but I hated everything else. I felt stuck. I drove my car all over the place for them with no reimbursement because the church was a financial mess, and on top of that, I could never quite excel in the church because I was a woman and I was just tired of doing it.

One night, before yet another church function, I looked at my boyfriend, who I now hated with a burning passion, and out of nowhere just said, "I'm done. This is over." Devin was stunned. What's funny is the way he tells the story now, it was a mutual breakup, but that's not true. I asked him to leave my house.

It took about a week for him to do some over the pants making out with another church girl in town, and then a few weeks after that, he met his now wife. She's a great singer and perfect for Devin because she's passive and loves the idea of being a preacher's wife. That thought always made me want to wretch.

Even though Devin had moved on in his relationship, and I was steadily gaining weight, he still called me multiple times a week just to talk. He wanted to "stay friends." It was too hard to deal with. This went on for a couple years until I worked up the courage to tell Devin never to call me again. I was finally able to turn away from him and the church he was a part of, and I haven't looked back.

Devin lives in a different state now with his wife and one million kids and is the youth pastor of some mega church and he makes these corny promotional videos and people believe that he is what he says he is, but I know better. He's a manipulative piece of shit that likes to hear himself talk. He always will be. Totally wish him the best though.

The point is, it's hard to let the worst people in your life go. From start to finish, I'd say this guy ruled my thoughts for around 6 years. SIX. When I finally got the nerve to end it, he had left a path of destruction in his wake. Thank god he met and married someone because who knows if I would have stuck to my guns.

Because of the cheating, I had developed trust issues that I thought were beyond repair and I had a body that was sick from being too heavy. My mental and physical health had been destroyed. I hated myself because I knew it was my fault. I had alienated all of my friends, and for financial reasons, I had moved back in with my parents. It was not a pretty sight.

I tried to cling to the spiritual life I had developed to get me through. In some ways, it did help, but I felt betrayed by the church in more ways than one. The sexism and racism filtering through each sermon and living inside the congregants made me wary of the church I had been attending. My faith was being chipped away.

Instead, I got through with the help of my friends. I started partying again. Most importantly, my friendship with Jordan deepened, and I credit him with saving me. I was at an emotional rock bottom, and without Jordan, my life would be completely different in a bad way.

I had finally drained the swamp of the people who were toxic in my life and filled it up with quality people who didn't suck the soul right out of my body like a dementor.

Since then, I've had to remove others from my swamp and some were just as difficult, if not more to remove. Sometimes, your family or coworkers are toxic. For those, you just have to weigh your options. Talking with those people or doing your best to find a new job may be your only choice. Be patient and diligent but keep draining.

It took me years to recover from that relationship. The combination of the ramifications of that breakup and my doctor warning me I would have diabetes by the time I was 30 if I didn't make some changes was what prompted me to get my shit together in the first place.

One of those steps was surrounding myself with supportive people and removing those who aren't. For the most part, I feel like I've found a good balance. I have people now that don't care what I weigh, think I'm beautiful at every number but still encourage me to succeed in all the financial, physical and career goals that I have. Do your best to get that too. It's a key step in changing your life!

Dive into Better Waters (Yummy Seafood Recipes)

Tuna Steak

I first fell in love with tuna steak when I ordered it on a whim at a Chattanooga restaurant. They no longer offer the dish, but it changed my perspective entirely when it comes to tuna. I had always eaten canned tuna as a child and enjoyed it, especially with a ton of mayo mixed in but a tuna steak is a whole different experience. If cooked properly (which means barely at all), tuna steak resembles actual beef. It's tender and juicy and delicious! I've cooked mine a variety of ways, but I love it with an Asian flare.

Ingredients:

- 1 tuna steak (I find these on sale at least once a month around town and stock up)
- 1 tablespoon toasted sesame oil
- 1 tablespoon toasted sesame seeds (neither the oil or the seeds have to be toasted, it's just my preference)
- 1 tablespoon soy sauce
- 1 tablespoon Teriyaki sauce
- Salt, pepper, garlic powder to taste

31

Directions:

Sprinkle the tuna steak with salt, pepper, and garlic powder.

Marinate the tuna steak in the sesame seeds, soy, and Teriyaki sauce for around ten minutes.

Bring the oil to temperature in a non-stick skillet. When the pan is at a medium-high heat, add the tuna steak.

Wait about 2 minutes and then flip it over. Let it cook for two minutes on the other side.

Then it's done. Tuna is best served rare, but if you like it overdone, that's your business.

I like to then slice it and serve it on a salad. I add more sesame seeds, chopped green onion, an oil and vinegar-based dressing, and if I'm being real outrageous, chunks of blue cheese. It's light and decadent all at the same time.

Catfished

I never imagined myself being the type of person that would eat catfish that wasn't breaded then deep-fried. My pro-tip here is that if you aren't going to fry the fish, don't skimp on the quality. I always assumed that all fish smelled like fish but when I buy catfish now, it's the fresh, best catfish I can find, and it doesn't even have a trace of fish smell. So, now, catfish is something I have as a luxury, which is also something I never thought would happen.

Ingredients:

- 2 fresh catfish filets
- 1 tablespoon toasted sesame oil
- 1 tablespoon soy sauce
- 1 tablespoon Teriyaki sauce
- 1 large zucchini
- 2 tablespoons chopped peanuts
- 2 servings rice (any kind you like)
- 1 tablespoon sesame seeds
- Green onion, pepper, garlic powder, salt to taste

Directions:

Marinate catfish in sesame oil, soy sauce, teriyaki sauce, garlic powder and pepper.

While that is marinating, cook your rice. (I like to make it easy, so I use frozen sushi rice. It cooks in no time and comes out perfect. I always screw up rice, so it's my short cut.)

Take a little more sesame oil and sauté the zucchini that you've sliced, salted, and peppered. I add a little garlic to the zucchini too. Once it's soft, take it out of the pan and set aside.

Put the marinated catfish filet in the hot skillet. You want about medium heat and a non-stick skillet. It only takes a few minutes on each side, so if you cooked your rice by boiling it, make sure it's almost done before putting on your catfish.

Mix the rice with the sautéed zucchini and put it on a plate.

Take one of the filets and place it on top of the bed of rice. Add chopped peanuts, sesame seeds and sliced green onion to the top.

The fish will be flaky and yummy and will pair nicely with the rice.

Tuna Tacos

As I mentioned previously, Tuna steak is a gift from the sea. Overcooked tuna turns into canned tuna and that's not what you're going for when it comes to tacos. If it's not overcooked, it's tender and moist almost like an actual steak. Also, keep a watch for it to go on sale at specialty stores. It can happen and when it does, grab them up and freeze them so you can have the decadence of tuna tacos anytime you want. I used to think the idea of a fish taco was disgusting but I've changed my ways.

Ingredients:

- 1 tuna steak
- 2 small (taco sized) corn or flour tortillas
- Shredded lettuce (you can also use fresh shredded cabbage but it's just not really my bag)
- 1 tablespoon ginger sesame salad dressing (or any Asian-inspired dressing you want. There are a lot of options these days in stores)
- 1 teaspoon garlic chili sauce (more if you want a kick)
- 1 clove minced garlic
- 1 tablespoon mayonnaise
- 1 teaspoon Sriracha sauce
- 1 tablespoon chopped peanuts
- 1 tablespoon toasted sesame seeds
- 2 tablespoons reduced fat Blue Cheese
- Green onion, soy sauce, salt, pepper, and garlic powder to taste

Directions:

Add salt, pepper, and garlic powder to both sides of tuna steak after patting it dry with a paper towel.

Marinate it in ginger dressing, chili sauce and minced garlic. While that's marinating, chop the lettuce, green onion, and peanuts.

Also, in a small bowl, mix together the mayo and Sriracha.

Bring a non-stick skillet to medium-high heat. Take the marinated tuna and sear on both sides for no more than 1-2 minutes per side.

As soon as a very thin white layer creeps up into the pink of the tuna, it's DONE.

When it's done, take it out of the pan and let the steak rest while you prepare the tacos. Take each tortilla, divide, and smear the Sriracha mayo on the bottom of both.

Add lettuce and blue cheese to each one. Sprinkle the chopped peanuts to taste.

Slice your tuna steak into strips and divide them evenly on each taco.

Sprinkle green onion and sesame seeds onto both tacos.

I put a few drops of soy sauce on each. I have a big appetite and two tacos fill me up. These tacos are hearty, salty, filling, and delicious.

Bang Bang Shrimp

Ingredients:

- ½ pound shrimp (peeled and deveined...tails are optional, but the flavor stays better if you leave them on)
- 2 tablespoons of low fat mayo
- 1 tablespoon of garlic Chili Sauce (you can find any variation of this that you like at your local store
- 1 teaspoon Sriracha sauce
- Chopped green onion
- Toasted sesame seeds
- Salt, pepper, garlic powder to taste

Directions:

To prepare the shrimp, season them with salt, pepper, and garlic powder. Throw them on the grill or sauté them in a skillet with about a tablespoon of toasted sesame oil.

While they are cooking (and it doesn't take more than a few minutes on either side), grab a bowl, and mix together the mayo, chili sauce, and Sriracha sauce.

When the shrimp are done, toss them in the sauce. Place them on a plate and top with chopped green onion and sesame seeds. This shrimp is good by itself or you can add it to rice or a salad.

Nothing excites me more on a menu than seeing key phrases like "Bang Bang" and "Uptown." I know that means I'm going to get a classic sweet and spicy combination!

Almond Crusted Fish

Ingredients:

- Any nice white fish. I used Alaskan Cod for this because it was on sale.
- 1 tablespoon olive oil.
- 2 tablespoons crushed almonds
- 2 tablespoons Dijon mustard
- Salt, pepper, garlic powder to taste

Pro Tip: I use a food processor for crushing almonds. You can chop them with a knife but make sure you chop them finely.

Directions:

This one is so easy. Heat the olive oil on medium heat in a non-stick skillet. While that heats up, pat your fish with a paper towel to get out any excess moisture. Add salt, pepper, and garlic powder.

Coat your fish in the Dijon mustard. (I personally like a pungent Dijon, but you can use a milder one if you like.)

Once the fish is coated in the mustard, cover it with the crushed almonds. Make sure every part of the fish is coated in both almond and mustard.

Then, just cook on each side about 3-4 minutes. I like to serve this with asparagus or on top of a salad.

3
CTFD

My friend Jordan and I have a short-hand language that includes a number of abbreviations. Sometimes, our abbreviations and acronyms sweep the nation, but we never get credit for them. Basically, we are emperors of wit, and we get no respect for anything.

Before I became a full-time teacher, I was stuck at a desk all day every day for seven years. Jordan is also forcibly attached to a desk each day but the perk of both our jobs at that time was that we could communicate via instant messaging every day. Since I'm no longer employed by my former company, I find it easy to admit that I spent a lot of time communicating via Messenger. Because Jordan is still working for the same company he was then, I will just say we only communicated in case of emergency.

During those years of messaging, one of the abbreviations that became commonplace was, "CTFD." This stands for, "Calm the fuck down." I mean, it's a phrase that can be used for any number of scenarios. Coworker being an asshole? In your head, you can be like,

"She needs to CTFD." Something juicy happen on *Scandal*? "Shonda Rhimes needs to CTFD." You get the point.

For me, I find myself needing to CTFD on a regular basis, especially when it comes to what I'm eating. One of my favorite books on the subject of dieting and weight loss is, *Breaking Free from Emotional Eating*, by Geneen Roth. In this book, and many other books she's written, Roth body slams the idea of traditional dieting. She is really, really against being on a diet, y'all. While reading it, I'm all, "Hell yes. Dieting is the worst! I'm never doing it again!" Then I proceed to eat an entire pizza because diets be damned!

I like to use Roth's words to justify certain foods sometimes. In reality though, her ultimate message is to eat what you want, when you want and stop when you're satisfied. When we diet, our mentality is that there's a list of foods we can have and a list of foods we can't have. When we go on a diet, we tend to think that we will never be able to have another piece of chocolate cake again, so in turn, all we can think about is said piece of cake. Whereas, if we eat cake when we want to without feeling like we are "cheating" somehow, we will stop at only a couple bites of cake as opposed to plowing through three pieces. Make sense? I think it does.

I've actually tried this too. I was all, "I'm going to stop counting calories and points, only eat when I'm hungry and stop as soon as I'm satisfied." The first day I nailed it. I was being cognizant of what my body was telling me. In addition to only eating when you're hungry, Roth also argues that we shouldn't eat mindlessly. So, no eating in the car, no eating standing up or while you're reading or watching TV. The idea is that if you sit down and it's just you and the food, you can appreciate it instead of swallowing it whole without tasting, the way dogs eat.

Like I said, the first day went off without a hitch. Then, as the week progressed, I began ignoring my body and mind. I was eating while distracted again and stuffing my face with whatever I wanted because Geneen Roth said it was OK. This is why mentality is the key component to any diet or non-diet for that matter. As Walter (played by John Goodman) in *The Big Lebowski* says, "This is not 'Nam... There are rules." There are *always* rules. Weight Watchers isn't perfect. Even though they argue you can eat what you want, it's not always true.

There are some things that the diet gods will always frown upon. For instance, sometimes a pile of chicken wings with ranch dressing is the only thing that will make me happy. Let's just say I have five wings with one side of ranch or blue cheese dressing. I'm looking at my entire allotment of points and/or calories for the whole day...not to mention the fact that I'm still hungry after I eat it. Some foods are just too delicious and full of fat to fit in on a diet.

Geneen Roth would argue to get the wings because she fancies herself a rule breaker. But that's the thing. There are instructional portions of her books with lists and numbers. You know what you call a numbered list of instructions? Rules. Even a book bashing traditional diet rules has its own set of guidelines (and promotes ridiculously expensive conferences to teach you how to "Break Free from Emotional Eating").

The ultimate goal is to find a balance between eating healthy and eating happy. I once heard someone say that you need to eat healthy 75% of the time. This is probably a solid rule, but it's one that is not only hard to quantify. Also, this rule is one I can manipulate in a hot second. Some people consider pasta salad with olives, olive oil, feta, bacon and avocado as healthy. "Ohh, it's got all these healthy fats and the pasta is gluten free! I'm being soooo

41

healthy right now." Um, guys, I hate to break up this party, but just because something has the word salad in it doesn't mean it's healthy. Trust me, I wish it were

Chicken salad loaded with mayo and cheese and whatever else southern people like to stuff into the word salad is delicious, but I'm not naïve. Oils and fats are still oils and fats. What's worse is that those "healthy" peanuts, avocados and olives are super fattening. It doesn't mean they are bad for you. There are plenty of health benefits in the "good" fats but eating a cup of pasta salad can't be added to the healthy list. And that's what I do. I take something pure like an avocado, add bacon and onion to it, mush it up to make guacamole and then add 30 tortilla chips and pretend I'm a beacon of health.

Maybe the idea is to find a happy medium between a restrictive diet and Roth's idea of eating whatever you want. Maybe we should stop categorizing foods into the "good" column and the "bad" column. We know what we *should* be eating. We know anything which leaves an orange, powdery residue on our fingers isn't ideal, but we should also stop berating ourselves for having the occasional cheesy puff.

Weight Watchers meetings can be corny as hell, but they can be useful. In addition to the accountability of weighing in each week in front of others, meetings are full of ideas and hokey inspirational quotes. Over the years, I've found that the most encouragement comes from the attendees and not the leaders. There's nothing wrong with the way leaders speak or run things, but everything they say has a corporate edge to it. The realest people are the ones getting up every Saturday morning to tell their stories of struggle or triumph.

One of the most valuable things I've ever heard someone say in a Weight Watchers meeting was, "Be your own best friend." She said that if your best friend called you and told you that she gained a pound, you wouldn't start yelling at her on the phone. You wouldn't call her worthless or a failure or tell her that she isn't really a human being because of a certain number on the scale. So, if you wouldn't tell your best friend that, then why would you tell yourself that?

It's so true. It's often said that we are our own worst critic. When it comes to body image, this seems especially accurate. If we go into a shame spiral every time we have a bite of junk food or eat one too many croutons on a salad, we are only emboldening the idea that diets are ultimately a prison and we are serving a life sentence.

For example, let's say you are on vacation and someone suggests that awesome breakfast buffet with the omelet station. In your head, you feel ready for it. You're going to have an egg white omelet, steer from carbs and eat lots of fruit. Before you know it, everything is a blur and you've eaten five pieces of bacon. Now you hate yourself. In your head, you've gained 20 pounds and you're an unlovable slug who should have known you'd fail. Why do we do this to ourselves? It's your vacation. Eat the fucking bacon.

The dynamic of success vs. failure in the diet world doesn't allow for anything other than perfection. Success equals following every rule without faltering and failure is anything other than that. Because we are human beings, we will repeatedly "fail" when the parameters are strict thus making us feel like failures. Not only do we feel like failures with our bodies, we project that mentality across the board. "Oh, I can't have a salad without dumping ranch dressing all over it? I probably won't ever publish a book either and I'm definitely never going to be on tenure track at school."

Listen to me. Eating 10 peanuts instead of 5 has absolutely no bearing on whether or not you get that promotion at work. It's important that you know that. It's important that *I* know that.

Dieting becomes an obsession so even when you are "successful," your fear of once again becoming a "failure" shrouds your ability to think straight and enjoy life.

There are folks out there who swear by food planning. They make it look so easy. These perky men and women poke around their kitchen in fitness gear for hours on Sunday preparing their four tablespoons of whole grain rice, six florets of broccoli and three ounces of boneless, skinless chicken breast and they say things like, "Eat to live don't live to eat." This is a judgment free zone. I don't intend to knock anyone for how they choose to stay healthy. As for me, over planning my food makes me an insane person, as does the monotony of having the same meal every day for weeks at a time.

When it comes to food and exercise, change is critical for me. Eating the same foods and keeping the same fitness routine for too long causes my goals to get derailed. Don't get me wrong, I do my fair share of planning. I plan mostly when I know I'm going to want to drink alcohol or I know I'm going to have a heavy meal the next day. I will try and minimize lunch if I know dinner is going to be caloric. I think doing the meal planning I see on the Internet would send me into a mental tailspin I'm not sure I would be able to get out of.

While my food planning may be limited to making a couple extra chicken breasts on the grill every week, that doesn't mean I don't obsess over food all the time. There's a reason my therapist was skeptical about my counting calories or points. It's an all-consuming process for me that causes stress and fuels the flames of my Obsessive-Compulsive Disorder.

I have known I had Obsessive Compulsive Disorder since I was 15 years old. OCD is defined by WebMD as "a potentially disabling illness that traps people in endless cycles of repetitive thoughts and behaviors. People with OCD are plagued by recurring and distressing thoughts, fears or images they cannot control." This illness can create a mountain of anxiety that some people express through rituals or routines. This is why so many people associate OCD with hand washing but that is a narrow scope of the disease itself.

My goal early on in high school was to get a scholarship to college. I knew my parents could never fork out the cash it would take for me to go to school. I wanted to avoid student loans if possible (the loans came later when grad school charged me out of the ass). So, I was juggling school, work, and the debate team (which was my key to a scholarship). I had the same struggles many kids my age did, but I haven't always been able to cope with stress well. I'm efficient and productive under stress but in my mind, I'm a hot mess.

Science has come a long way in determining that there doesn't have to be a *reason* to feel anxious. A panic attack can come out of nowhere. Back then though, a cry for help was seen as weakness. Most people felt that a teen my age who had a roof over her head and a solid family shouldn't have to worry about anything. Luckily, even though there's still a stigma associated with mental health, it has gotten better.

Because I didn't know any methods to deal with the anxiety I was having, I started developing some odd habits. I feel that I need symmetry so everything I did on my left side had to be done on my right. For instance, I wear the same amount of jewelry on each hand. If I have a watch and a ring on the left, I will put two bracelets on my right hand. Not only that, when I was done showering in high school, I would place my hands under the faucet and alternate them back and forth. So, I'd bend over, stick my right hand in the water one second, then my left and then I'd repeat that process multiple times until I felt like I could stop.

I also started counting. I count when I clap, take stairs and when I adjust the volume on the radio or TV. Everything needs to be in 5s and 10s. After college, when I was still trying to maintain a spiritual life, I started praying for every person I knew by name every night before bed. I felt like if I didn't pray for them, they would die. I've always had horrific images of my family members dying so out of nowhere I suddenly felt that the power to control their safety and health was in my hands. I used to wake up in a panic and run to my little brother's room to make sure he was alive.

I don't do the prayer or shower thing anymore. I still count everything in 5s and 10s, and now, I obsessively check irons (hair and clothes), ovens, candles, and the lint trap because I'm scared of house fires. I have horrific nightmares sometimes and in addition to dreaming about the death of loved ones, I often dream about being engulfed by water or a natural disaster.

So, even though I am a hypochondriac, I felt it was pretty safe to diagnose myself with OCD. When I started therapy, I told her that I had it and she wasn't dismissive but was more like, "I'll be the judge of that." It didn't take long for her to officially tell me I could say I was OCD.

I feel incredibly grateful that my OCD rituals are small and don't have a major impact on those around me. The worst part of my OCD would be intrusive thoughts. In fact, that's how she determined I had OCD in the first place. She said that obsessing all day every day about the same few areas of my life was actually a symptom of my OCD and not anxiety but that the effect of those thoughts could be anxiety and depression.

I never in a million years thought that I would get anything out of therapy. In some cases, it's exactly what I thought it would be. It's a repetitive cycle of me spewing about my issues and her suggesting a new kind of meditation she found on YouTube. Sometimes that stuff works and sometimes it doesn't. What I've found most helpful is learning that there are many layers of anxiety and OCD. Knowing that there is a reason for thinking certain thoughts allows me to pinpoint specific issues and work on them one at a time. The ultimate goal is to think less, but so far, I just think more and now I'm thinking about thinking.

All of that probably sounded like a jumbled mess and I apologize. I guess it's important for me to reiterate that when I'm all, "You need to calm the fuck down," I'm also talking to myself. The problem is, it's not always easy. In life, someone is always expecting you to do something. Whether it's your employer, family, friends or yourself, there are always needs that need to be met.

Life is a constant process of being pulled in a thousand directions. For me, I rely on my planner for everything. It reminds me to grade papers, keep appointments and even water the plants. Actually, to say I rely on it is probably an understatement. It is my security blanket. If it's not on there, I didn't do it, and/or it doesn't exist. So, when I add counting calories or points to my already jumbled brain, it can sometimes make my OCD and anxiety worse.

If I'm on an official diet, I am consistently thinking about my next consumption of food or drink, no matter how big or small. I'll use up my points at night and as I go to bed, I'm wondering what I will have for breakfast and how much it will set me back.

I want eggs, but I better only have one piece of toast because I'd like to have bread at dinner. Oh, and I'll need to save for a snack. Or would I rather have a glass of wine? But I bet I'll be hungry if I do that. Maybe half a glass tomorrow night with a small piece of dark chocolate.

That is an example of my stream of consciousness. This is no way to spend well deserved down time. This is where balance and Roth's idea of eating when you're hungry comes in. Overthinking every detail about your day and week right down to what you are going to have lunch three days from now is enough to put anyone in a padded room.

Let's try something different. If you're reading this (I'll do it too). Mark where you're at in the book. Close your eyes and take ten seconds to take a deep, slow breath in. Fill up your lungs with air and count all the way to ten. Then, release that breath just as slowly. Open your eyes.

Any time you feel like your thoughts are so overwhelming that they may begin to seep out of your ears, nose, and mouth, take a deep breath like that. I'm going to try to do it too.

As a woman, I know all too well how annoying it is for someone to tell you to calm down. Sometimes, life's chaos can't be helped. What we can do is chill about the small stuff. A decision on whether or not to include low fat mayo on your sandwich shouldn't be one that you wrestle with for ten minutes or ten seconds for that matter. Your life is far more precious than that, and so is mine. So, let's all CTFD.

Calm Down & Have a Calorie-Friendly Cupcake Y'all!

Semi-Homemade Diet Cola Cupcakes

I've tried a lot of sugar free and low-sugar desserts, and most of them are terrible. I didn't invent diet soda cakes by any means. I've seen them everywhere. However, I have come up with several combinations and ideas when it comes to them, and I have found them to be a suitable alternative when your sweet tooth won't leave you alone. Also, I make all of these in cupcake form because of portion control and cuteness factor, but they work as a whole cake as well.

Chocolate Cola Cupcakes

Ingredients:

- 1 box of your favorite chocolate cake mix
- 12 ounce can of diet cola
- 1 tub light whipped cream
- 1 tablespoon of chocolate fudge topping (out of a jar is fine)

Directions:

Pre-heat the oven established on the instructions on the back of the cake mix box. Empty the box of cake mix into a mixing bowl, add soda. Mix.

Pour the mixture evenly into a 12-cupcake cupcake pan that is lined with liners and sprayed with non-stick spray. Bake the recommended amount of time on the box.

While the cupcakes are baking, get out another bowl and mix together the chocolate fudge with the whipped cream.

Cover and refrigerate. When the cupcakes are done, let them cool completely if you want them to have the frosting.

Kick it up a Notch: Adding a frozen, miniature peanut butter cup to the middle of the batter before baking makes the cupcake even more decadent, and they will still have fewer calories than a full-fat piece of cake.

Pro tip: Only frost the cupcakes you want at that moment. If you frost all of them and refrigerate, the top gets a bit gummy. Frost them as you eat them.

Variation1: Creamsicle Cupcakes

Directions: Follow the directions above, but swap in the ingredients below for these quick and easy variations on a delicious treat!

Ingredients:

- 1 box of your favorite vanilla or yellow cake mix
- 12 ounce can of diet orange soda
- 1 tub light whipped cream
- Zest of one orange
- Juice of one orange

Pro Tip: The zest and juice are optional but add a really bright orange flavor. You'll be able to taste the orange in the cupcakes, but it will be somewhat faint so adding the extra to the frosting will really amp up the orange vibe in the cupcake.

Variation 2: Ginger and Spice Cupcakes

Ingredients:

- 1 box of your favorite spice cake mix
- 12 ounce can of diet ginger ale
- 1 tub light whipped cream
- 1 teaspoon cinnamon
- 3 servings of very thin gingersnaps, crushed

Black Forest Cupcakes

Ingredients:

- 1 box of either dark chocolate or fudge cake mix
- 12 ounce can of diet cherry cola
- 1 can of cherry pie filling (no sugar added)
- 1 tub light whipped cream
- 1 bag of mini chocolate chips (Put in the pantry what you don't use)
- 1 jar of Maraschino cherries

Note: Many of these ingredients are optional and affect the calorie count. You can skip the filling and toppings, but putting it all together makes a more authentic (and delicious) black forest cake.

Directions:

Follow the directions above. Pour the mixture evenly into a 12-cupcake cupcake pan that is lined with liners and sprayed with non-stick spray. Open the cherry pie filling, take a teaspoon, and place a small dollop of filling into the center of each unbaked cupcake.

Bake. When the cupcakes are done, let them cool completely before adding frosting. When you are ready to eat one, add the whipped cream and top with a mini-chocolate chips and a cherry.

Pro-Tip: This recipe also works brilliantly with strawberries! Just replace the cherry pie filling with strawberry pie filling, and it tastes like a chocolate-covered strawberry!

Strawberry Shortcake Cupcake

Ingredients:

- 1 box of yellow cake mix
- 12 ounce can of diet cream soda
- 1 small jar of reduced sugar strawberry jam or jelly
- 1 tub light whipped cream
- 12 fresh, small strawberries

Directions:

Follow the directions above. Once everything is mixed, pour the mixture evenly into a 12-cupcake cupcake pan that is lined with liners and sprayed with non-stick spray.

Open the strawberry jam, take a teaspoon, and place a small dollop of filling into the center of each unbaked cupcake.

Bake. When the cupcakes are done, let them cool completely before you add any frosting.

You can either frost each one with whipped cream and then add a whole strawberry on top OR you can chop the strawberries up, add them to the cream and then frost them that way.

4

Sorry Not Sorry

As a 33-year old woman living in Tuscaloosa, Alabama, I should be married, own a home and be raising 2.5 kids and a dog right now. Or, at least that is what southern society would have me believe.

There is always pressure from society for us to behave a certain way. It's why so many people have a difficult time telling their parents they are gay or dating someone outside their race. It's why people judge working mothers or those who only go to church on Easter and Christmas. It's why so many people have difficulty accepting the bodies they were born with. Over the years, society has placed certain parameters on every aspect of life. When you step outside those parameters, there are people there to judge your every move.

For example, when I wasn't married by the age of 25, my grandmother suggested that I try eHarmony in front of my entire immediate and extended family. There was this assumption that I was some lonely spinster who was either a lesbian or a chubby, unlovable bitch who couldn't find a man. Sure, those words may seem harsh, and certainly my grandmother would never say the words bitch or lesbian out loud, but those of us that have been there understand this feeling. That feeling is that the people who are most important to you don't feel like you're doing life the way you *should* be doing life.

When I was in college at the University of Alabama, I was majoring in Secondary Education. I wanted to be an English Teacher. Because my math and science skills were lacking, as was my desire to try to excel in those subjects, I had some issues with my GPA. I was still on scholarship and things weren't as dramatic as they seemed, but it was looking like getting into the education program was going to be a difficult task.

My debate coach advised me to major in the subject that interested me the most and figure out the teaching part later. He said that pinning myself to a trade like teaching would box me in to one area. This made total sense to me and though it's been a difficult road, he was right. I'm where I want to be in terms of my career.

So, a few semesters into my college career, I changed my major to American Studies with a minor in Creative Writing. You can imagine what it was like giving my parents this nugget of information. Their shining star who basically made high school her bitch was now a mediocre college student who wanted to get a degree in American Studies, and what the hell does that even mean?

This is a bit narcissistic to say, but my parents raised two fairly responsible, intelligent children, so whenever we (but especially me) did anything less-than exemplary, it seemed as if the world was falling apart.

My parents developed a "as long as you're under my roof" attitude once I graduated high school. It seemed like it came out of nowhere, and I didn't react by abiding by their newfound fascist regime. Instead, I declared an all-out war. I was an adult after all and they couldn't tell me what to do.

We fought constantly during that time. I'd tell them I would rather find the nearest abandoned cardboard box to spend the night than live with them. They would question every move I made and threaten to cut me off financially.

Looking back on those times, I'm still often labeled the two-headed, devil-like, teenage villain that was the source of all the drama. I'll take my share of the credit, but my parents weren't perfect either. I was made to feel guilty for everything. All in all, I was a good kid. I just don't think my parents knew what to do with their first child who was seeking freedom and putting up a fight every step of the way.

I don't have children of my own, but my brother is ten years younger than me and I see him make the same sly moves that I sometimes used to make. When I was a teenager, I wasn't capable of perspective. It was apparent to me that the only goal my parents had was to unequivocally ruin my life. I know now that's not true.

Since those days, I feel like I've been trying to make up for those times. I try everything in my power to please my parents. My innate need to make not only them happy, but also everyone else around me happy, is a crippling truth that I am working to resolve.

I spent several years defending my decision to get a degree in American Studies and then a Masters in Writing, but why?

Part of the problem is that while many of us don't follow the rules laid out by society, they are still entrenched in us so when we make a choice that steers from the norm, we question it right along with everyone else. Deep down, we feel there's a chance that the haters are right.

One of the biggest mistakes we make is failing to trust our own instincts. Being scared to tell your parents you're changing your major is understandable but deciding not to change it because you are afraid of what they will think is no way to live a life. I say that, but I'm still terrified to tell my mother I won't be able to make it to Sunday dinner if a friend is having a birthday party.

Guilt is a powerful emotion. It energizes anxiety and makes people do any number of things they don't want to in order to make another person happy. There are people out there who should win awards for their ability to sling a guilt trip your way. I've been known to do it myself a time or two and let me just say, I get it honestly.

Life is hard. Helping folks out in their time of need and occasionally doing something when you'd rather be in bed with no clothes on watching *Chopped* is one thing but totally rearranging your life on a daily basis out of guilt or fear of upsetting someone else is a tragic way to spend your life.

Remember in the movie *Love Actually* when Laura Linney gives up the hot guy to take care of her mentally ill brother? Remember thinking how stupid she was? I mean, you understood that her bro needed help but that he was also in a facility being cared for and that she was living her whole life either in the workplace or visiting her unwell brother and she *needed* to bang that hot guy. Because I'm the kind of person that thinks about fictional characters as real people, I sometimes think about Linney's character in that movie and I want to smack her across the face and tell her to live her life!

58

Then sometimes, I remember that I can't say no either. I will do whatever, whenever to avoid the guilt. What's sad is I'm only that fervent with those who are the most difficult to please. I tend to put the patient and understanding people to the side who won't make me feel guilty for taking too long to respond to a text or not wanting to get out of the house on a Saturday morning for a non-emergent event. It's the people who are most patient and understanding that I should be catering to, but instead, it's the other way around.

I will read a text conversation I've had with someone 100 times to see if there's something I could have said to upset them. I will reference a comment I made a month prior to that and apologize about it just in case it made them angry.

Now, there are people in my life who are demanding for sure, but much of it is my inability to let things go...keep calm and carry on and all that. It has never been easy for me to not worry about the things I can't control. I worry about everything all the time.

When I first moved to Tuscaloosa and was made aware that it had both giant cockroaches and tornadoes, I spent many nights, tossing and turning, worrying that a roach would crawl on my face or a tornado would sweep me away.

One book I read on anxiety called *Monkey Mind* by Daniel Smith said, "like a hermit crab stripped of its shell, my anxiety went looking for another home." My brain will always have something to overthink and oftentimes, it's about whether or not someone is mad at me.

While I am not sure I'll ever be able to nonchalantly accept that a friend is miffed about something I've said or done, I can work on saying no. I can work on not being sorry for living my life.

When I was a kid, I taught my stuffed animals English. I cut my Barbie's hair on "salon day" and made her and Ken "do it" in the pink limo. I rode my sweet, neon pink bike that had the AM/FM radio on it. I watched *Grease* every afternoon. I did a lot of things. One thing I never did: think about my future wedding and having lots of children.

I had way too many careers I had to excel at first. If I was going to be a teacher, actor, lawyer, and doctor, I had no time to worry about a family. It is true I've always wanted to be a teacher, but I found other careers attractive as well.

I've never been fond of children. Since I helped take care of my brother, I know how gross kids are and how high maintenance they can be. When you have a kid, you bring another human being into your life that can't perform basic human functions. They need you for everything. I've never found this appealing. Why on earth would I try and take care of a child when I'm still on my mom's car insurance at the age of 33? That just seems silly and irresponsible.

Having said that, I'm also the kind of person that doesn't say "never." As gross as this will sound, I've done things I never thought I'd do since meeting my boyfriend, Ian. If you tell anyone this, I will kill you but a year (Lies! It was a month) into my relationship with him, I set up a wedding board on Pinterest and a note on my phone that said, "Future I Do." Barf. Also, the idea of pregnancy doesn't horrify me as much as it did before I met Ian.

The worst part about having "future" feelings and discussions about a stupid boy is that I feel like my family walks around with this smug, "I told you so," look on their faces like they just knew I'd come around to the "traditional" lifestyle eventually. I still reject the fact that anyone *needs* someone else to be happy and

I am 1000% sure that it's totally possible to live a fulfilling life without having children (if that's your choice).

Having said that, I find myself all domesticated, living with my long-term boyfriend and my dogs, excited because I have an eggplant purple Kitchen-Aid Mixer. It's a little more difficult now to rage against the machine when I ask for a vacuum for Christmas, but I still try.

The point is, fuck what everyone else thinks. How do you want to live your life? Don't apologize for who you are. That includes your sexual orientation, race, job, choices, relationship status (even if there isn't one), and whatever else you decide. Sure, if you're 40 years old, three months behind on a bill and just asked your mom to pay for it, skip out on that cross-country road trip to the Coors' plant in Colorado. Let's not get out of control with the "sorry not sorry" mentality. However, if you're someone who works hard and wants to love who you are what you do, don't give that up just to please society or someone in your family. You are so much better than that. So am I.

On top of that, let's stop apologizing on a daily basis for our beliefs and choices and Facebook statuses.

Some people see everything in black and white. Only republicans can support troops. Liberals are a godless bunch who would be totally fine with a rabbit legally marrying a four-year old child. There are folks out there who are this extreme on both sides. My Dad fancies himself in the category of middle ground but doesn't always prove that when he speaks. What I find most annoying is that my parents, along with many others within a decade or two of my age, seem to feel that my generation are entitled sacks of shit who think we know everything. What's funny is that my parents taught me to be smart and independent. My parents hounded my ass about homework since my first year of school and it was my mother who encouraged me to be on the debate team. What did you expect? You pushed me to learn, to explore and now you're all, "Oh, you think you're sooooo smart, don't you?"

As a lover of the former Aaron Sorkin show, *The West Wing*, I often quote it. Sometimes, Martin Sheen, or President Bartlet would get push back from his staff for being "too smart." They felt it made him seem out of touch to every day voters. So, thus the quote, "Let Bartlet Be Bartlet," was born. I'm not sure why but there seems to be an influx of hostility towards the educated.

It's actually an age-old problem. I teach American literature nearly every semester. There are a string of stories from writers like Cather, Twain and others who explore this idea of the educated versus the non-educated but in the age of social media, those themes play themselves out on a daily basis on a Facebook status thread. It is entirely possible for a college graduate to be friends with a hard-working high school dropout guys. Just be respectful of each other. Have empathy.

The point is, we often shy away from our real feelings in order to make sure we aren't making anyone angry. If your neighbor down the street can say that he believes our former president has ties with ISIS in a Tweet and the pretentious snob you went to school with can write a think piece about *his* thoughts on solving patriarchy in the country, then you can say what the hell you want when the hell you want to.

How does this tie into mental and physical health? It's simple. When we are over-apologizing for who we are, what we do and the things we say on a constant basis, we are waving around a flag that says, "I have no confidence!"

62

Nobody likes a know it all but as I tell my students, "You are a human being with valid opinions. As long as you back those opinions up with logic and fact checking, you are allowed to voice those opinions."

If we say we are sorry for a tone we may have accidentally used in a text or for speaking up in a group conversation, we will never have the confidence it takes to take care of ourselves. You are important enough to believe that you have the strength to accomplish anything you want, and you don't have to apologize for shit. Once you realize that, it's much easier to take time out for yourself.

Guilt-Free Family Favorites

You don't have to let family expectations define you, but you can honor your heritage & traditions by cooking your favorite family recipes. Here are some of my favorites!

Mom's Best-Cheeseball-Ever

Ingredients:

- 2- eight-ounce packages of softened cream cheese
- 1 stick unsalted butter
- ½ cup sour cream
- 1 pound grated cheddar cheese
- ¼ cup grate onion
- 2 to 4 cloves of minced garlic to taste
- Salt, pepper, and Worcestershire sauce to taste (probably around 2 tablespoons)
- Around 2 cups chopped pecans
- Crackers of choice

Directions:

Begin by adding butter, onion, and garlic to a food processor first so the onion and garlic are smooth.

If you have a small food processor, it's easier to prepare the mixture in two batches.

Next, add the cheese and sour cream. Once all the ingredients are combined, taste it to make sure it has the right amount of salt, pepper, Worcestershire sauce and garlic.

Take the mixture and in a medium-sized bowl, formulated in a ball. Chill until firm (best if overnight).

Once the mixture is chilled and can be handled, coat the ball in the pecans that you can spread out on plastic wrap.

Serve with the crackers of your choice (buttery crackers are the best).

Pro Tip: You can also take square wheat crackers and make it look like a turkey on Thanksgiving... but that may be a funny family tradition only our family likes!

Grandma's Sauerkraut & Weenies

Ingredients:

- 4 hot dogs (any brand you choose, you could go lean, but it's your choice)
- 1 tablespoon bacon grease (Listen, everything at Grandma's house was cooked with bacon grease)
- 2 to 4 cups sauerkraut (You can buy this or make your own. Grandma makes her own)
- Salt and pepper to taste

Directions:

Heat the bacon grease in a non-stick skillet on medium heat.

Add sauerkraut and stir until cooked through.

Add in chopped "weenies" and when they are cooked to your liking, you are all ready to go!

Dad's Favorite Omelet

My mother is most definitely the cook of the family but that doesn't mean I don't have great memories of my Dad and. My most distinct memories are from childhood. My mother worked several jobs at a time, so we could make ends meet. That meant that there were nights my Dad was in charge of cooking.

We ate a lot of Hamburger Helper in those days and to be honest, I could live the rest of my life without having another box of that stuff. He also made breakfast occasionally. He'd make pancakes in the shape of an "H" and on really special days, he'd make me an omelet.

I'm an egg fan and omelets are great because you can toss whatever you want in them. My Dad's has a key ingredient that many people don't use, and I wish they did: sour cream. It isn't exactly the healthiest omelet in the world, but boy, is it good.

Ingredients:

- 2 eggs
- 3 tablespoons of sour cream (you can feel free to use Light)
- 1 tablespoon butter
- 2 tablespoons of milk
- ¼ cup shredded cheddar cheese
- 2 pieces fried bacon (crispy)
- 2 pieces deli ham
- Sliced green onions for garnish
- Salt, pepper, garlic powder to taste

Directions:

Heat butter in a non-stick skillet on medium heat. While butter is melting, whisk together eggs, milk, salt, pepper, and garlic powder.

Add mixture to skillet and let it sit until it's done on the bottom.

Once the egg easily comes up from the bottom of the pan, flip the omelet over (you may need more butter or seasoning depending on your taste).

After it's flipped, add cheese, bacon, ham, and sour cream to one side.

Wait about 1-2 minutes and fold the omelet over. Don't let it cook too long or the eggs will get dry and the cheese and sour cream will get too melty.

I like when the sour cream is still cold and thick because I have a sour cream problem.

Mom's Spaghetti and Meatballs

(For Special Occasions Because This Crap is Labor Intensive)

Ingredients

- 1 box Angel Hair pasta
- 1 pound lean ground beef
- 1 pound ground pork
- 2 medium onions (Chop one and grate the other)
- 2 tablespoons parsley
- 2 tablespoon oregano
- 2 tablespoon Italian seasoning
- 2 teaspoon basil
- 2- twenty-nine-ounce cans tomato sauce
- 12 ounce can tomato paste
- ½ cup dry red wine
- 4 ounce can mushrooms
- 4 cloves garlic minced
- 5 mozzarella string cheese sticks, cut into fourths
- ¾ cup Parmesan Cheese
- 10 saltines, crumbled (or, you can use breadcrumbs)
- 1 egg
- ¼ cup milk
- Salt and pepper to taste

Directions:

Preheat oven to 350. Take ¼ of the ground beef and ¼ of the ground pork and brown in a skillet on medium heat. Drain grease.

Add chopped onions and half of the garlic and brown that also.

Add a tablespoon of parsley, oregano, Italian seasoning, and basil to the pan while it's still frying and add drained mushrooms.

Add sauces and paste and then add the wine with about ¼ cup water to the tomato sauce can and add to the pan in order to retrieve all of the sauce.

Simmer the sauce 2 hours on low heat. While the sauce is simmering, prepare your meatballs.

Add remaining pork and beef to large bowl, add remaining minced garlic, salt, and pepper.

Then add a tablespoon of parsley, oregano, Italian seasoning, and basil to the bowl.

Grate an onion into the bowl. Add Parmesan cheese, saltines, egg, and milk.

Combine ingredients with hands. Take a glob of the mixture (about the size of the palm of your hand) and put it in your palm.

Press a divot in the middle and add a piece of string cheese, then add meat on top of it so you have a ball and no exposed mozzarella cheese.

Add meatballs to cookie sheet about an inch and a half apart and bake them for 20-30 minutes.

Halfway through the baking process, turn them over.

When meatballs are finished, go ahead, and add them to the simmering sauce.

Don't over stir the sauce! Once the meatballs have been added so you don't break them apart. Once the sauce is finished, serve over pasta.

Tater Tot Casserole

Ingredients:

- 1 pound lean ground beef
- 1 onion, chopped
- 2 cloves garlic, minced (you can use garlic powder also)
- 1 bag frozen tater tots
- 1 to 2 cups grated sharp cheddar cheese (we always go a little heavy on the cheese)
- 1 regular size can cream of mushroom soup
- 1 eight-ounce tub sour cream (or more if you're in the mood)
- Salt, pepper, garlic powder to taste

Directions:

Preheat the oven to 350. Season beef with salt and pepper. Brown hamburger meat in a skillet on medium heat, breaking it up as it cooks. Once it's cooked through, drain the grease from the skillet.

Add chopped onions and garlic to the pan and let them soften. Place the hamburger mixture in a 9x11 baking dish and spread the can of cream of mushroom soup on top.

Then take the sour cream and spread it over that.

Spread tater tots evenly on top of the mixture then sprinkle with salt, pepper, and garlic powder. Add shredded cheese.

Bake for 30 minutes.

71

5

YOLO

Yes, I said "YOLO," y'all. It just seems appropriate for this section. In the same vein of over-apologizing, it's also important that you are confident enough to think you can reach your goals in the first place. Excuses are the number one reason people give up their dreams before they ever really get started.

I once had a conversation with someone in a tumultuous marriage who said that she would never leave her husband because she was too old to start over. She also felt that she couldn't sustain her lifestyle with her children financially if she left. Now, I'm not dumb enough to suggest someone leave his or her spouse. I don't need that kind of baggage in my life. Having said that, I did tell her that her dependence was self-inflicted. I told her that leaving her husband was a decision that she would have to make on her own but that there was no reason she couldn't try to map out ways to become more independent.

In another example, I was discussing books I'd read with a coworker when another coworker chimed in with disgust, "How on earth do you have time to *read*?" Instead of asking her why the thought of other people reading made her so upset, I simply told her that I made a choice to read for at least a few minutes every day because I think it helps me become a better writer.

It didn't stop there. "Well, I have kids and I don't have time to read. I collapse in my bed at night. Must be nice."

Y'all, I just love being shamed by mothers for not having kids. The funny part was that the initial coworker I was talking to before she added her two cents, who also reads books, has kids.

It would have been easier if she had just said, "I don't like reading." Instead, she acted like taking 15-20 minutes a day to read in order to enrich my life was an assault on her hers. "You could make time to read if you wanted to," I wanted to say. She finally admitted she didn't like reading, but her initial response to the fact that I make time to read every day was hostile and defensive.

This is common too. When people feel bad for not doing certain things to improve their life, they immediately begin a laundry list of the reasons why they don't do them. As someone who puts her daily struggles of healthy living out there where the world can see, I often find myself in conversations about other people's health choices. I'm not super comfortable talking about my weight, what I eat or how I feel about my body with other people, but I understand that because I write about it, people may ask. So, when it happens, I engage.

The way people approach me is a bit odd. For example, when I'm trying to be more health conscious with my food decisions, people notice. I used to prepare a thin bagel and light cream cheese almost every day at my old job. I will give a hypothetical example of a typical interaction. Someone is grabbing a honeybun out of the snack machine as I'm making my breakfast. Let's say I'm standing there, quietly spreading exactly one tablespoon of light cream cheese on either side of the bagel. The person at the snack machine will turn around and say something like, "I've had a stressful week." At first, I won't know they are talking to me. "That's why I am having a honeybun."

There it is. It's apparent now that this person wants me, and everyone else on this planet, to tell them it's OK to have a honeybun. So, I will give them what they want. "Oh, I understand! Eat that honeybun."

They will stand there staring at the honeybun, contemplating every life decision they've ever made. "I wish I had time to bring my breakfast like you do," They'll say. Sure, you and I have such different lives that I have all of this luxurious time in the morning.

"I just bring a bag of bagels with me and keep the cream cheese in the fridge," I explain.

Then they are all, "Well, not all of us have your will power," and storm out of the room. Before I know it, eating a fucking thin bagel has made someone feel bad about their entire day and possibly even their life.

Now, obviously, my food choices aren't always within the parameters of what the diet gods allow and maybe I should have said that to the honeybun-eating coworker. What I feel is the more pressing issue is that this person has their own set of problems that prompts them to make excuses about what they are doing.

A common excuse people use has to do with age. People simply believe that they are too old to make changes in their lives, so they stay stagnant and complacent. What people don't know is that age doesn't have to be a preventative factor in life. There are people missing out on phenomenal lives out of fear that they are too old. This is upsetting to me.

In 2015, *The Huffington Post* reported that Georgina Harwood, a woman from South Africa, spent her 100th birthday skydiving with plans to scuba dive with sharks. In December of 2016, *The New York Times* printed a story about a man named Ed Whitlock from Canada that is an 85-year-old marathon runner. He's a marvel of a physical specimen. Finally, *USA Today* reported that a 99-year-old woman named Doreetha Daniels graduated from College of the Canyons in Santa Clarita, California with an Associate's Degree in 2015.

Now, these are inspirational stories, but they are extreme cases and I'm not suggesting that you create some outlandish goal of walking a tightrope between two skyscrapers on your 70th birthday but the point is that you shouldn't let age, or any other excuse stop you from doing what you want to do.

When it comes to health, people are ready and willing to make excuses. I'll be the first to admit that I blame anything I can think of as a justification for decisions I make about my health.

There are two components to this. First, I don't think I should have to make excuses for being overweight and you shouldn't either. I often make self-deprecating jokes or use my thyroid as an essential apology for being fat. I know I'm not supposed to use the F word but there it is. If I had a level of acceptance regarding my body, I wouldn't feel the need to make excuses for it.

The second component is that I am simply coming up with reasons to have a weekend binge, or drink a third margarita or eat a giant piece of chocolate cake. It's OK to do those things sometimes but getting at the crux of *why* I do that seems like the most important part.

Another reason people reject the notion of change and refuse to fulfill their dreams is because of fear. The fear is generally that of failure. This is my primary method of excuse making and it happens most in my stream of consciousness. I don't submit my writing to a number of contests because I automatically conclude it's not good enough. I don't apply for certain teaching positions because I feel I'm unqualified.

I'm not alone in this. People turn down jobs, decide not to move, stay in a bad marriage, and in general, neglect to make changes in their life because they are scared to fail. We have all been victims of this mentality. As a whole, we need to stop making excuses and start making smaller, more attainable goals and chip away at our fears and do the unthinkable.

When I was working in the corporate world, getting harassed about honeybuns, all I wanted was to do was teach. I had gotten my Master's and I was ready to use it. It is not easy to get your foot in the door when you start teaching. So, I applied every month (or at least that's what it felt like) and sent multiple emails to the woman in charge of scheduling classes. I even made a couple personal visits. Apparently, I was annoying enough to make my name pop up in her head when they were in desperate need for a teacher to fill a section.

Just like that, my foot was in the door. It took a long time and when I first started teaching, I was terrified. I was thrown into the position without much training, and without the two friends I had in the department to lean on, I would have been screwed. Now, I am a full-time teacher and even though I'm poor, I couldn't be happier with my career choice.

If you're thinking about making a major change, as long as it is healthy for your body, there's no reason to wait until Monday, or next week or next year. Make a choice today.

One of the primary ways to make changes, as I've already said, is to make small, attainable goals. If you're a numbers person, remember, you can't lose 50 pounds before you lose 5. I repeat that phrase a lot. I'll talk about the importance of exercise overall later but when I started on my journey to get healthy, I didn't exercise at all. One of my proudest accomplishments was taking myself from a five-minute walk a day to running a half marathon.

Sometimes people make the mistake of jumping in headfirst. You see this happen on shows like *The Biggest Loser,* but this is real life. You have to do something that you can commit to. If you are extremely overweight and haven't exercised in multiple years, you can't expect to run a marathon in a week.

I am not a doctor but there is a reason that almost every fitness program or exercise machine says to check with your physician before you begin anything. You have to make sure your body is equipped for what you are putting it through.

Also, like dieting, exercise is a mental game. If you go from doing nothing to saying you're going to try to jog a mile and do 45 minutes on the elliptical on the first day, you may get it done but you'll be so exhausted and sore that you may skip one or two days in a row or even worse, never go back. Then, you may say to yourself, "Well, I tried. Forget it."

If you start slow, and I mean really slow, it's hard to have an excuse not to do what you said you were going to do in the first place. As I already mentioned, when I first started exercising again, I promised myself I would walk 5 minutes each morning before work, taking Saturday and Sunday off. 5 minutes sounds laughable, right? Well, I was doing nothing before, so I was going from no movement to 25 minutes' worth of walking a week.

Within two minutes of walking on the first day, a bead of sweat landed on my brow and what felt like an open sword wound assaulted my rib cage. I had second-guessed my decision to begin exercising almost immediately but kept going.

The house I lived in at the time was centered in between a couple of hills so it wasn't the easiest five-minute walk in the world. After the first day, I was a bit fatigued and a little sore. I can't really describe how out of shape I was but perhaps you have an idea if I was sore and tired after a five-minute walk. The thing was though, it only took five minutes out of my day and I wasn't hurting enough to give up.

The next day, I went out again. This time, it was a little easier. This went on for a few weeks. After I had mastered the five-minute walk, I decided I would step it up a notch. I changed it to ten minutes a day. It was a simple change in some ways. I didn't add anything fancy, but I was doubling the amount of time I would walk in a week.

Again, I've never really enjoyed exercise, but these morning walks are a fond memory for me. Not only was I beginning an exercise journey that would eventually exceed everything I thought I could be capable of, but I was also taking time for myself. Each morning, for ten minutes, I put on headphones and got to know myself better. Sometimes we get so caught up in the details of the

79

day that we don't take a moment to breathe and examine who we are.

Each morning that I got up and walked, I was accomplishing something. I was knocking out the doubt little by little. I progressed fairly quickly and was walking enough to challenge myself to walk 1 million steps in 130 days. It was something that several people at work were doing with pedometers they gave us as an insurance incentive. This seemed like a big challenge, but I found myself excited at the prospect of walking a million steps. When I look at my Nike app now and see that I've traveled well over 500 miles on foot the past couple years, I feel an enormous sense of pride. The million-step challenge was one of the first goals that I achieved that gave me motivation. I ended up exceeding the million-step goal and it was at that point I decided to do something I never thought I could: run.

The embarrassment of the physical fitness test is one of the most painful and vivid memories of high school. We had to take these challenges each year to see where we stood compared to the average teenager. The two most horrifying tests were the chin-ups and the mile run. Everyone stood in a group and watched as one by one we went up to the rusty pull up bar to see if we could use our arm strength to pull ourselves up in the air. The goal of course is to go high enough for the chin to go above the bar.

Obviously, I couldn't do this. The good news was that at least half the class couldn't do it, and one of the most popular guys in school farted in the middle of *his* pull-ups. I was already self-conscious so taking my chubby high school body up to the bar was terrifying. I would wrap my fingers around the bar and pull with all my might. All eyes were on me, and I could hear a couple sniggers going around the group. It occurred to me that high school must be designed to teach you how to deal with humiliation. I was never able to do a pull up and I can say with a great deal of confidence that I couldn't do one now, though admittedly I haven't tried since my teenage years.

The other challenge was the one-mile run. It's so funny because in hindsight, one mile is really not that bad. I just assumed I couldn't do it, so I made a mockery out of the whole thing. I remember both PE teachers I had in high school as if it all happened yesterday. The first was an older man. He was grumpy and wrinkled and only referred to students by their last name. Hearing the angry, "Wyatt!" used to send chills down my spine.

He was there the first time I had to run the mile. As the whistle blew, I attempted to jog for a few seconds but realized quickly I wasn't going to be able to do it. I could hear him screaming at me to hustle from a distance. I began to walk, feeling immense pain in my side. 48 minutes later, I was on my third lap when he finally made everyone come in.

The next year I had to run it didn't go much better. My PE teacher that year was a woman with short, curly, black hair and masculine features. She was about 4'11" and a bit pudgy. She was nice to you if you used your car to go get her breakfast but mostly she was just crabby. If you asked me, she looked exactly like a thumb. The truth is, these people could be perfectly wonderful, but I have negative associations with high school and exercise.

This time I decided I wanted to do a bit better so once again, I started strong. I might have gone ten seconds but stopped when my shins felt like someone had just taken a mallet to them. When I passed by her on my way back around, I would jog a bit as I went by, so she would think I was trying. Somehow, when I was finishing my third lap, she thought I was done, so I managed to finish my "mile" in under 30 minutes. She let me know the time was terrible, but little did she know that I was only 75% done.

So, when I considered running for the first time in my adult life, the idea seemed ludicrous and brought back a slew of painful memories. Then I thought, you know, in this time in my life I'm accomplishing things I never thought I could. I was losing weight left and right, walking over a million steps and getting a Master's degree. Maybe I *could* run. It was something I wanted to try.

I started by downloading an app called Couch to 5K. I had heard of people having success with this app and the name sounded promising. After finishing the program, I didn't completely agree with the notion that one could literally go from being a couch potato to running a 5K, but the important part was that it started you off slowly. Most of the workouts take 20 to 30 minutes. The idea is that in 9 weeks, you are able to run a 5K without stopping in 30 minutes.

I wasn't too worried about how quickly I was running, especially since I was a beginner. On the program, you run three times a week and the first week has you alternating walking and jogging. You never jog more than 60 seconds at a time in the first couple weeks. If I've heard the phrase, "You can do anything for 60 seconds" once, I've heard it a thousand times. Honestly, it's kind of a mantra for me. I tend to agree. I won't lie, the first time I ran for a whole minute without stopping, I was worried I might die. I know that sounds dramatic but it's true.

My train of thought:

This hurts.

OMG my ribs hurt. I wonder if that's normal.

Holy shit, my shins. OH MY GOD MY SHINS!

Can you break a shin?

My lungs hurt.

I hope I don't have a heart attack.

For the first several weeks, I had this circle of thoughts on repeat. There was nothing comfortable about running. It hurt my knees, shins and affected my breathing. About half way through the program though I was still alive and could run 5 minutes without stopping. This was, for me, a profound achievement. I had never run more than a few seconds at a time in my entire life. Also, even though running still hurt, it wasn't quite as bad. I was actually able to think about things other than my pain.

I finished the program and though I couldn't run a 5K in 30 minutes, I could run 30 minutes without stopping.

I decided I was ready for my first 5K. 5Ks have been popping up everywhere in the past several years as a popular way to raise money. It's not difficult to find one. I signed up for a 5K at Kentuck Park in Northport, Alabama. While I don't mind exercising at the gym with others, I have never really cared for running with anyone. I feel like I need music and complete focus, so I signed up for this one by myself. The morning of the race, I was nervous. I didn't really feel like running to be honest but 5Ks cost money and I needed to prove to myself that I could do it.

I was there early and saw the crowds of people. I went to the tent to get my packet. Packets are great by the way. If you're into T-shirts and coupons from local businesses, packets are the best part of a race. Each time I run in an event, I take a great deal of pride pinning a bib to my shirt. As a writer I'm always looking for symbolism and it doesn't get much more symbolic than pinning a race bib to your belly when you're on a weight loss journey. I took a deep breath. I was ready.

I assumed I was beside the start line but about fifty yards away I heard some shouting and a buzz and quickly realized that the race was starting without me and I was nowhere near the start line. I started my first 5K about 3 minutes later than everyone else did. This was not really the news I needed but I wasn't there for anyone but myself, so I proceeded. I began jogging at the start line and pretty much stayed solo the entire time. I had my music going and began thinking of the beer and snacks at the finish line.

It took me nearly 45 minutes to complete my first 5K. That is certainly not the best time in the world, but for me, it felt like an amazing accomplishment. I was totally exhausted and sore after the first time, but I was eager to sign up for another one. Over the next couple years, I ran in several 5Ks. I ran in what Tuscaloosa calls the Mayor's Cup, color runs, glow runs, mud runs and each time, I would get better and better. My fastest one-mile run was 10 minutes and 54 seconds. I insist on giving my dog credit for that time. I don't usually take him running with me because he's insane on a leash but one day I wanted to run a quick mile and brought him with me. He pulled me along and even with his 100 quick stops to pee, I still beat my record time. I'm not much for running fast but admittedly, I was proud of running a mile in less than 11 minutes. I haven't done it again. My fastest 5K was 35 minutes and 27 seconds which averages out to about 11 minutes 23 seconds per mile. I felt like I could take my new ability to run even further.

It was at that time that I decided to run in the 2014 Tuscaloosa Half Marathon. At that point, my longest distance was about a five-mile run but I had learned to pace myself and I thought the half marathon would be a fantastic goal. I was terrified at the thought of it but deep down, I felt like I could do it. I downloaded an app on my phone called the 21K trainer. Just the thought of going from a 5K to a 21K was enough to freak me out but I wanted to try. I've never had the best knees, so I was concerned. My mom was also concerned. I could tell by her face that she wasn't sure it was the best idea. Naturally, I wanted it even more since my mom didn't want me to do it.

I began my training using the app and it was quite a change from the couch to 5K training I had done years before. The training program is 12 weeks so that's how much time I gave myself. The first day of the 21K training program has a five-minute warm up walk followed by a 60-minute run. I feel like they do this on purpose because a 60-minute jog is not easy. In fact, it's really hard. Right away I was pushing myself because I was meeting, if not exceeding, a distance I had only done once before. It wasn't like this every time. I was given days when you only had to run 30 minutes but as I progressed in my training, the dreaded weekly "long run" would just get longer and longer.

By week 7, I was running 90 minutes at a time. The only downside to the app was that while it prepared me for a long run, it assumed that by the end of it, I was running 13 miles in 2 hours. As I said before, I'm not a fast runner. I would start off with an average of 11 minutes a mile, then as I got further in the run, I'd slow to 14, 15, or even 16 minutes a mile. Really, before the half marathon, I had only run about 9 or 10 miles. It wasn't a true preparation for over 13. There were many times during that 3-month period where I really questioned my ability to run the entire way. People kept telling me that it didn't matter how much time it took or if I decided to walk some of the race, but I knew that if I stopped during the half marathon at all, I wouldn't be able to make it the rest of the way.

85

About ¾ of the way into the training, I was nearing the end of approximately an 8-mile run. In Tuscaloosa, it takes a bit of creativity to run 8 miles without repeating your setting. I ran down a hill located on campus and I was nearing the road by the river. I was almost done so I ran a bit down that road and then turned around. It was my longest run at that point, so I was exhausted. When the voice on my headphones told me I could stop running, I halted abruptly. When I did, my knee locked up and decided it was done working for the day. I felt a shock of pain go through my entire body, starting at the knee, and working its way both up and down my legs. I thought I was going to throw up for a second. I stopped what I was doing and finally got my leg to work again. I felt a throbbing pain as I tried to walk it out and I started to cry.

I felt like such a baby but the pain in my knee worried me. I was afraid I would have to stop running for a few days, that I would get behind on my training, and that I wouldn't be able to run the half marathon.

I can't believe you ever thought you could do this.

I wiped the tears from my eyes mostly because I was worried that someone would see me crying. I began a downward spiral mentally that involved quite a bit of self-loathing.

I should mention that at the time, I thought I was the only person in the world who had ever trained for and ran in a half marathon and *gained* weight (though I hear now that it's not uncommon). Every time I got done with a really long run, I was ravenous. If I ever train like that again, I know I need to have food on deck that I can destroy immediately because back then, I would scarf down food from the closest place I could get it and it wouldn't always be the healthiest.

Because of these cravings, I put on a few pounds in the process. In short, I felt too fat to be running in a half marathon. The whole experience taught me a lot about what to eat and not eat before and after working out. It's important to eat protein and carbohydrates for fuel but it's also important not to gorge yourself after a hard workout. Smoothies and energy boosts like Spark are great for these moments.

The next morning, I woke up and my knee didn't have any lasting pain. This was both a burden and a relief. In some ways it would have been easier if I had no choice but to give up. On the other hand, I knew that an injury would be not only a waste of an entry fee, but I also feared it would be a gateway to weight gain. I told myself that from now on, rather than stopping my runs on a dime, I would slowly come to a pause. This small change made a world of difference. I have always had joint pain when I run, especially in my knees and hips. But it's pain I can live with nothing a little Icy Hot can't fix. I want to push my body as long as I can. I know my limitations and there are some things I can't do but I *knew* I could do this.

The week before the half marathon was easy physically because the goal is to taper your runs. I was nervous though and felt this cloud of dread. I just wanted it to be over with. The day before the run, I enjoyed eating pasta for lunch and rice for dinner. It's rare to get two carb-y meals when you're on a strict diet but I read that people carbo-loaded prior to runs and I was most definitely on board that train.

The morning of the run, I was on my own. It felt lonely but not in a bad way. I wasn't completely alone, as there were thousands of other people, but this journey was a solo one and even though I had support, I knew it was up to me to finish. I stopped by

McDonald's and had an Egg White Delight and some apple slices on the way. One of my fears was that I would need to pee during the race, so I tried to ration my fluid intake. I also made sure to visit the port-o-potty several times before it started.

I did my stretching. I copied the most fit-looking runners on their stretches for time and structure because I figured they knew what they were doing. I tied my shoes tight, stuck my energy gel, keys, and phone in my fanny pack, started my playlist (which is extremely important), took a deep breath and stepped up to the start line.

I had a mix of music that some might find strange. There were Broadway show tunes from plays like "Les Mis," "Wicked" and "Hairspray." I also had a combination of pop stars like Katy Perry, Taylor Swift and Pink. I had Eminem for when I felt invincible. Then, when I needed to slow down, I had more laid-back female artists like Ingrid Michaelson and Sara Bareilles ("Chasing the Sun" is one of the best running songs ever). I suppose everyone's playlist is different but music, for me, is of utmost importance when running, otherwise it's just the sound of my heavy breathing and pounding feet and heart.

The shotgun went off. For a moment, we were all a group, a cluster of "runners" heading for the same goal. It didn't take long for the group to separate. We became speckled dots all over the roads of Tuscaloosa. We started our run at the Tuscaloosa Amphitheater, the place we'd also end up. We headed up the river and took a right to go into the downtown area. It took less than half a mile before the trail took us up roughly the third steepest hill downtown, beside a barbecue joint. I'm not sure what type of sadist makes runners embarking on a 13-mile run go up a hill all whilst smelling the natural perfume of a smoking pig, but I have been meaning to write a letter about that for a couple years now.

There are a lot of ugly characteristics in the world of modern technology. Social media has allowed the ignorance of people you went to high school with and family shine brightly for the whole world to see. However, there are some fun attributes that make it all seem worth it. For me, the most exciting part about the existence of social media while running in a half marathon was the ability to take pictures and videos on my phone as I was going and text/Snapchat them to my friends. I will admit that distractions while running tend to slow me down but in the moments that I was snapping videos and pictures, I wasn't thinking about how far I had to go and moments like those are all too precious in the middle of a 13-mile run.

I won't say the first few miles were easy, but they still held the motivation and adrenaline that appeared when the gunshot started the race. There were mile markers and water stations, but I found the most motivating aspects of the race were the people planted at different points to cheer you on. I never imagined that I would like having a group of sorority girls or a high school marching band clap for me and cheer me along but I found it comforting to know that they were there. I'm not naïve enough to think that they were there out of the goodness of their hearts. I know that they were fulfilling some type of philanthropy requirement, but I didn't care if they were rented out, I needed them.

I ran all over downtown and then the race took us to campus. I am more than just an alumnus or someone who is affiliated with the University of Alabama; my life is completely intertwined with the institution. My father has always been an Alabama fan, I have lived in Tuscaloosa since I was 12, I graduated from Alabama, I've attended every home game for years and I am now an English instructor there. So, running by the stadium and other assorted campus landmarks gave me the comfort of familiarity. I found the signs that some of the volunteer cheerleaders funny and encouraging, especially ones like "I'm tired just watching you."

About halfway through the race, I was deep into the campus, which is a bit hilly. I rounded a corner, passing a building I regularly teach in and suddenly I was faced with a giant (it felt giant) hill in front of me. It was at this time that words of encouragement I kept repeating to myself turned into curse words that would make a sailor blush. Another hill? Really? I used to live in Chattanooga as a child so in comparison, Tuscaloosa seems like a flat landscape and I suppose it is but it sure as hell didn't seem flat that day.

While I was running slowly up this hill I remembered someone telling me they walked the hills when they ran their half marathon. This seemed tempting. I also started to forget how far I had come and began only thinking about how far I had to go which was a dangerous shift in mindset. I gave myself a pep talk and kept chugging along. By the time I threw my mental tantrum, I was up the hill, and everything started to get a bit better.

Finally, I reached Campus Drive. Once I made my way up this road, I would turn left on Helen Keller, then left onto Jack Warner Parkway which would take me all the way down the river to the finish line. The Campus Drive hill wasn't steep, but it was by far the most torturous stretch of the whole race. It was a steady incline for what felt like an entire mile. I decided that I missed the short, steep hills because having this long of a stretch that inclines was cruel and unusual punishment.

The guy that sold me my tennis shoes was in charge of cheering people up this hill. I saw him, and I knew my face was contorted in pain. He could sense this and said, "You're almost done, I swear." I wanted to believe him. I did. But this was the moment I started to break emotionally. This was the moment I had serious doubt I was going to finish. I only had a few miles left, but running 3 miles is hard enough, and running 3 miles after I had already run 10 seemed damn near impossible.

There was a water station coming up so before I got to it, I reached in my fanny pack and grabbed my energy gel. It came in my race packet for free. I never tried it before but thought it would be worth a shot. I pulled the foil pack out and ripped it open with my teeth. I squeezed it between my lips and a hot swirl of strawberry gel filled my mouth and taste buds. The gel must have been 100 degrees and as I tried to swallow it, I thought I might throw up. I noticed the port-o-potties to my left. I needed to pee a little and thought maybe I could break, use the restroom, get some water, and spit this heinous gel out of my mouth.

Suddenly, the thought of stepping foot into a hot portable toilet made my need to heave my guts out on the side of the road grow exponentially. Instead, I took my swig of water, sloshed it around my mouth and spit out the remaining gel. I turned the tiny paper cone up into my mouth, cherishing the few drops that came out and kept going.

I had made it to the river. If I could just keep going, I would get to the path I've taken a hundred times and I would make it. I took a video of myself just repeating the phrase, "Lord, please carry me down this river."

I am sure there is a psychological reason why the last bits of a run are the absolute worst. You've told your brain how far you need to run and it's like, "You're almost done!" The only thing is, it wasn't exciting. I wasn't to the point of smelling the finish line. I could feel pain beginning in the arches of my feet, creeping all the way up to the top of my head. It felt like each step I took, skin was tearing from my heels and someone was there to add an extra smash to the bottom of my feet with a hammer. My hips were on fire, I was gushing sweat, and I was nauseated.

I was in the final stretch. I had two miles left, and I wanted to quit so bad that I started to tear up. I try to act tough but this whole race thing was taking its toll mentally and it was all coming to a head. Then, at the last mile marker, something beautiful happened. I saw my coworkers.

This was before I was a teacher. These were the coworkers I had during my seven-year stint in the corporate world. Sometimes I really effing hated that place. There was always drama, the building was freezing, the work was mundane, people sneezed without covering their mouths, they would eat your lunch, and being there sucked the soul straight out of your body. That day though, when I saw them through the trees, I had never been happier to see anyone in my entire life.

They saw me and started waving. They had been looking for me! I managed to smile back and Calvin, one of my favorite people from the old job came to greet me. Calvin is one of the fittest people I know. He has a six-pack he loves to show off and he walks faster than I run. He kept telling me it was almost over and jogged with me for several feet. When he left me, I ran a bit further and within a few minutes I could actually see the finish line. There was no reason to stop now. It was within reach.

I ran up the final incline and headed toward the amp. As I got on the cement path, I had my final bit of encouragement. My father and my aunt were there, grinning ear to ear, running to catch me, both with video cameras in hand. My aunt's video would later show only a view of the grass, but it's the thought that counts. I will always be heart-broken for people who don't have support systems. Even when my people don't understand my decisions, or they don't agree with them, they love me and support me and damn, that feels good.

I saw my dad trip over something in the grass, and he almost came tumbling down as he was trying to film me. They were running with me. I couldn't help but smile. I rounded the corner and the finish line was less than fifty yards away. Luckily there were no crowds because nearly everyone had finished. I saw my brother standing behind a fence, also filming, also proud. Near the finish line I saw my Mom and my Oma beaming. I will never know but I'm not sure I could have finished those last couple of miles without all of the support.

I crossed the finish line and slowly came to a stop. I bent over, feeling what felt like an asthma attack coming on. For a few brief seconds, I couldn't breathe. Part of the problem was panic. Once I felt like I wasn't going to be able to catch my breath, I started worrying that something was wrong. Ultimately the problem was simple: I was worn slap out. I finally caught a breath and took the bottle of water that one of the volunteers at the finish line handed me. Even though the winners of the competition crossed the line more than an hour before that and probably already received their complimentary massage and barbecue sandwich, everyone was still cheering for me. After a couple swigs of water, I saw my Dad coming toward me, smiling broadly. He hugged me.

If you know me, you know I'm not a touchy-feely person. I value my personal space and it's not often that I embrace the idea of affection. Anyway, in this rare instance, I returned my Dad's big hug and tears welled in my eyes. I didn't want to be *that girl*, the one who becomes overwhelmed with emotion and cries because I finished a race. I mean, sure, I had jogged for over 13 miles without stopping but this wasn't the Olympics, and I wasn't Kerri Strug. However, I had set forth a goal and accomplished it and this time, the goal was really hard and took a toll on me both physically and mentally.

I pulled myself together and greeted the rest of my family. The finish line was located at the Tuscaloosa Amphitheater, which happens to be at the bottom of a steep hill. On top of that hill is downtown Tuscaloosa. I had already decided that I wanted my post-race meal to be at Mugshots, a burger joint in the heart of downtown. The problem was, none of the people I was with were able to park close to the Amp so in order to get to Mugshots, I had to walk up the steep hill to get to it. I thought I might actually cry again. I guess looking back now it's kind of funny that after running so far, I had to add just a little more insult to injury before I could eat my well-earned food.

This also happened to be the first day that my parents met my boyfriend, Ian. Ian is possibly one of the sweetest people on the face of the planet, but he's a bit shy, and all in one day, he was there to support me for the half marathon and he was thrown into a lunch with my entire family. Despite the fact that I smelled like a rotten goat and I annihilated all the calories I burned by stuffing a giant burger in my face, it was an amazing day.

A few days later, I received the results of the race. We wore a sensor in our bib to track our times and our place in the race overall. My time was 3 hours, 8 minutes, and 55 seconds. Though I told everyone my only goal was to finish, I had secretly hoped to finish in under 3 hours, so this was a little disappointing. It meant my average pace was 14:28 per mile. There are people that can walk a mile at that speed, so it meant I was going pretty dang slow at times. I convinced myself not to dwell on this detail.

I had completed the race and that was the primary accomplishment. I had to chuckle when it said that my overall place in the race was 865 (the 477th woman to finish) and that out of the 69 female runners from the ages of 25 to 29, I finished 63rd. In my mind I imagined that some of them probably didn't even show up or maybe they walked the whole time. A couple weeks before the race I had a recurring dream that I would be the last one to finish and by the time I got to the finish line everyone would be gone. I wondered how much longer I had before that dream became a reality. It was just like me to demean my achievement with technical details, so I laughed it off.

As recommended, I took some time off from running. The first few days I didn't run because I had no choice. I felt like I had been dumped in a garbage truck, shredded by a metal claw, and then compressed. I could barely walk, let alone jog. I wanted to make sure that I could still run so since then, up until the last year, I ran at least a few times a week. I was contemplating running in the 2015 half marathon, so I started long runs again and then did something nasty to my right knee that took me a couple weeks to walk off. I made the decision to focus on other forms of exercise. Even though I swore off running those big races again, I feel like I'll make a liar out of myself one of those days. I had never been so determined to complete a goal and the feeling of pride when I was done was so unbelievably strong, I might need another taste of it.

The ultimate point of the story isn't to tell you to run a half marathon. Hell, I'm not even suggesting you run. That was a personal goal for me. It was something I never thought I could conquer and to this day, I don't think I've been more driven in my life to finish anything else. My goal is to tell you that even me, someone who is an expert at half-assing and making excuses, set out for domination, and found success. It won't be easy. You will want to quit. You are strong enough to do anything you want. So, do it.

Post Workout Protein

Satisfying dishes to eat after you sweat!

Baked Chicken Fajitas for Two

I love Mexican food more than I love a large percentage of my family members. Nothing is better than dipping a fried tortilla into melted cheese and sipping on a sugary margarita. I eat a lot of Mexican food. I don't always succeed at staying healthy, but when I do, it's because I order simple.

Sometimes, I'll order "street tacos." They usually don't have cheese and are served on a corn tortilla with just onion and cilantro. Other times, I'll order fajitas. They can be oily, but if you skip the tortillas, sour cream and cheese and fill up on meat, beans, pico, lettuce, and salsa, you can feel full on fewer calories. Or, you can make fiesta night at home.

Ingredients:

- 2 large boneless, skinless chicken breasts
- 1 tablespoon olive oil
- 1 teaspoon chili powder
- 1 teaspoon smoked Paprika
- 1 teaspoon garlic powder
- 1 can of diced tomatoes mixed with green chilis

- 1 medium yellow onion, sliced
- 1 package sliced mushrooms (*note, this is optional. I include mushrooms because I don't eat peppers. You could leave them out and grab a green bell pepper if that suits your taste better)
- Salt, pepper to taste

Directions:

Pre-heat Oven to 400 degrees. Cut the chicken breasts into small strips. Grab a casserole dish.

Add the chicken, olive oil, chili powder, smoked paprika, garlic powder, canned tomatoes, onions, and mushrooms. Add salt and pepper.

With a pair of tongs, toss together all ingredients. Spread them evenly in the dish.

Bake the fajitas for 30 minutes or until chicken is cooked all the way through.

Serve alone or with all the fixins. In case you're curious, I think appropriate fixins for this dish would be: tortillas, sour cream, shredded cheese, salsa, guacamole and black or refried beans.

Steak Burrito Bowl

Ingredients:

- 1 small strip steak
- ½ cup cooked rice or Quinoa
- ½ cup black beans
- Grilled corn
- Salsa
- Lettuce
- Chopped onion
- Black olives
- 2 tablespoons light sour cream
- 2 tablespoons low fat shredded cheese
- 2 tablespoons guacamole (they now sell these in individually packaged cups and they are amazing)
- Salt, pepper, garlic powder, chili powder to taste
- Chopped green onions for garnish

Directions:

Fire up the grill. Add salt, pepper, garlic powder and chili powder to the steak and corn on the cob. Don't overdo it but you want a little kick.

Cook the steak and corn 3-4 minutes on either side and then let the steak rest while you prepare the other ingredients.

While those are cooking, prepare the rice (or go the easy route with microwaveable) and rinse the black beans (you can heat them you want but they are fine straight out of a can as long as you rinse off the juices).

Once the corn has cooled enough, slice the kernels off the cob. Chop the onions and the olives if you didn't already and then start assembling.

Add the rice to the bottom and then the rest of the order is up to you. Slice the steak before adding it to the bowl

This is unbelievably filling, and when you add a kick to the ingredients, it always feels like you are indulging.

Mediterranean Chicken

Ingredients:

- 1 grilled chicken breast
- 1 whole zucchini, sliced or chopped
- Half onion (chopped)
- 5 to 10 Kalamata olives, chopped
- 1/4 reduced fat free Feta Cheese
- 1 tablespoon light Balsamic Vinaigrette dressing

Directions:

Preheat oven to 350 degrees. If you have grilled chicken ready to go, that's great. If not, I recommend grilling the chicken and grilling the zucchini, too. It adds nice flavor.

If you have a grill pan, you can just dice it but if you don't, you'll need to grill it vertically in spears or halves. If you don't grill the zucchini, spray a non-stick skillet with cooking spray and add chopped zucchini and onions. Let them soften a few minutes.

Take a shallow pan (a cookie sheet or aluminum pie pan will work), line with foil and spray with non-stick cooking spray.

Add the chicken, and then top it with the zucchini, onion, and olives. Bake in the oven for 5 minutes. Bring it out, add the feta, and bake an additional 5-10 minutes.

When it comes out of the oven, drizzle the dressing on top. You can eat this by itself, but I've also had it on a salad and it worked really nicely that way as well.

Honey Soy Pork Chops for Two

Ingredients:

- 2 bone-in center cut thick pork chops
- 1 clove garlic, minced
- 2 tablespoons honey
- 3 tablespoons soy sauce
- 1 tablespoon olive oil
- Salt, pepper to taste

Directions:

In a bowl, mix together garlic, honey, and soy sauce. Take the uncooked pork chops and put them in the bowl, covering them with the marinade. Sit in the refrigerator for at least an hour but you could put them in their overnight.

Once they are marinated in the refrigerator, take them out and add oil to a non-stick, oven-safe skillet at medium-high heat. Also, pre-heat the oven to 350 degrees.

As soon as the oil is hot, add the chops and sear them for 2-3 minutes on each side.

Pop the entire pan into the oven for 10 minutes so the pork chops can cook all the way through.

This is great with a side of fresh green beans that you've also tossed in garlic, honey and soy sauce and roasted for 30-35 minutes.

6

Get Your Shit Together

Have you ever been asked the question, "If your house was on fire and you could only grab three things, what would you take?" For the past several years, I would say my number one answer to this question (without really even thinking about the other two items) would be: my planner. It's a sickness really but my planner means more to me than a lot of people that I know.

Each year, around November, I begin looking for the perfect planner. Because of the fantastic site, plumpaper.com, I now get the joy of building my own planner to suit my needs. My family and friends know the importance of the planner and know that I put everything I do in it. First, it helps me remember the tasks I want to do every day like write, grade, check my emails, etc. Second, I add other less strenuous tasks in my planner because it allows me to take my purple highlighter (I ordered a whole box of them on Amazon) and highlight what I've done. It feels good to check something off a list, even if it is just watering the plants or, you know, showering.

My heightened organization has gotten me in trouble with friends. They sometimes find my obsessive-compulsive need to write them into my planner belittling. I certainly don't intend to make my friends feel like just another part of my schedule, though I can understand that writing "Lunch with Jordan" next to "walk the dog" or "take trash out" can feel like I'm equating them to a menial task I have to get done. That's not the case. The planner is for me and has no bearing on how I feel about those I love the most. Also, it comes in handy because people have used my planner to trace a moment in time in their own lives. I've been able to figure out when certain fights have happened in relationships, when people died and when someone needs a haircut.

In this section, I'm not suggesting that anyone get a planner and become an insane person like me. If I'm being honest, my attachment to my planner is a borderline sickness. There has to be a happy medium between living by an organized schedule and having no sense of organization at all.

My planner represents a lack of clutter. I hate clutter. I am possibly the opposite of a hoarder. I've gotten rid of clothes, decorative items, cards, and a plethora of other things because they don't have a "place." If something doesn't have a place, it needs to go in the trash. Many people feel I get rid of things prematurely and maybe they are right but when I say, "get your shit together," I mean it.

When we think about overall wellness, both physical and mental, we don't always consider the stressful aspects of life that are taking up space in our already busy lives. I've already spoken about removing toxic people in your life but it's also important to remove other chaotic triggers keeping us from living our best life.

When deciding to clear out all the garbage, start with the physical clutter and it will trickle down to the mental clutter. You can begin this process of simplifying your life by taking a deep breath. Breathing is important. In fact, if you'd like, take a deep breath right now. I can talk more about breathing later but whenever I find life to be overwhelming, I take a long, deep breath. It doesn't solve everything, but it allows me to center myself and regain focus. Sometimes I need more than one big breath.

So, what in your life could use a decluttering? Think about your desk at work. Does it look like a model in a catalog with one pen and a perfectly angled keyboard? Or, does it look like an office supply store exploded and instead of seeing the bright, shining faces of your friends and family in frames, they've got post-it notes stuck to their heads with reminders to "get organized."

If you walk into your office every day, and there are heaping piles of paper everywhere and you call it "organized chaos," it can lead you down a dangerous mental path.

Perhaps your desk is clean. I mean, it is 2017 after all. Who still uses paper? Everything is on the computer. Perfect. The only problem with that is just because you have removed the physical clutter from your desk doesn't mean that all of that mess couldn't be transferred right over to a computer. Think about your desktop. How many folders do you have? How many emails are in your inbox right now?

Many of you are busy at work. Many of you are also behind at work. I'm not saying getting your shit together will be easy y'all. In fact, it's going to be really difficult. You may have to stay late every day for a few weeks. You might have to come in one Sunday to get it done but if you go in, and only work on the clutter and the mess, you can arrive one Monday morning and actually only work on the task at hand for that day. Imagine how amazing that would be.

What does your car look like? Are you the kind of person that is bogged down with clutter at work and then gets in the car and there are 47 water bottles, 16 cardboard fast food cups, paperwork that no longer fits at your desk, four purses, napkins, crumbs and possibly living creatures?

If you are that person, how can you possibly relax if there's this kind of clutter in every aspect of your life? You know that feeling of dread when the dishes in the dishwasher are clean and you would literally rather have someone sling mud in your face than have to dry the dishes? I do too. For some reason the most menial tasks are the worst for me. I *hate* pumping gas. Like, I know it sounds so grossly privileged to say but pumping gas disgusts me. It's boring, costs money and you have to deal with the elements of nature.

I also believe that because I hate it so much, the world punishes me by always leading me to a non-working pump or one that moves slow enough to make me feel like I'm dying on the inside. I don't love doing dishes either. I'll whine internally about it all day and then I'll find myself in the kitchen, without any excuses. Approximately 4 minutes later, I'm done unloading the dishwasher. I'll sigh with relief because it's done and then realize it wasn't so bad.

You'll find that once you bite the bullet on some of these things (i.e. your desk or car), it won't take as long as you think, and you will feel a huge sense of relief once it's done.

So, organize those folders, delete those spam emails (trust me, the woman from Russia isn't really interested in showing you a good time), chunk all the trash from your car and simplify your life. It's hard to take a deep breath when your surroundings are stealing all the best air around you.

One of the safest spaces on earth is supposed to be your home. In a perfect world, your house is a bubble where none of those heinous people from work, or awful worldly events, can get to you. You should be able to walk in your door, say hi to your dumb dog, remove your pants and bra, pour a glass of wine and binge watch a bad reality TV show without any distractions.

Unfortunately, we tend to muck up our safe bubble with clutter too and when we do this, there's no escape from the outside world. Now, as an exclaimer, I don't have children. So, before you get hostile and argue that I don't know what it's like, you're right. I don't. I can't imagine the amount of laundry folks with kids have to do on a weekly basis. I have two dogs and there is rarely a time when something is rotating in the washer and dryer. I also know there are appointments and practices and moments of crisis that I can't begin to understand.

There is always a reason why clutter happens. It still doesn't mean that removing it wouldn't be beneficial to everyone's mental and physical health. My suggestion would be to really dig deep and figure out a way to work on it. It may take months but doing one project at a time will make you feel like a superhero. Make a plan.

If you do have kids, you probably have a buttload (technical term) of toys and clothes they don't need anymore. If you don't have kids, well, you also probably have toys and clothes you don't need anymore. God, grow up. One of the first steps in getting your shit together at home can be having a yard sale.

You may not think you have anything worth selling but you're probably wrong. You'd be surprised how much someone wants the bobble head you won from a radio station. Not only that, you can gather your neighbors, family and/or friends and have a joint yard sale. Take one Friday night, grab anything in your house that can be sold and set it up on tables in your front yard or garage. Post the sale on social media and staple a poster to the light pole at the road and, "BAM," people will be at your house at 6AM on a Saturday morning. Whatever doesn't sell, take it immediately to a donation center so you aren't tempted to redistribute it back in the house. In one weekend you've made a little money and removed a ton of clutter from your house.

If you don't have time for a yard sale, you can, at the very least, get rid of some clothes. I have a bad habit of getting rid of things but there is one area that I am more stubborn: clothes. I have clothes of every size in my closet. I have clothes from when I was at my heaviest weight, clothes from my smallest weight and everything in between. On the one hand, it's nice to have a variety since I fluctuate so much. On the other hand, having clothes that fit is more than just a logistic. If your clothes are too tight or too loose, you won't ever feel confident in what you're wearing. I know how oppressive numbers can be.

There was a time when I was gaining weight and refused to move up a size. Because of that, I had no clothes that fit me. Therefore, I was wearing exercise pants or pajama pants everywhere I went. It's difficult to feel better about the way you look if you're always wearing an old t-shirt and pants, especially if the reason is that you don't have any clothes.

I decided that I would go get some new clothes, no matter what size they were. Once I did, I immediately felt better. I realized that I cleaned up pretty well even though I had gained weight, and having clothes and shoes that accentuated the right areas made me feel beautiful again. It's amazing what happens when you have a solid-fitting pair of jeans and brush your hair.

If your clothes don't fit, donate them. Your closet needs to be a place where you can waltz right in, throw on any outfit and feel ready to dominate whatever the day brings you. If you're low on cash, try selling some of those "skinny" clothes from your college days that do nothing but remind you of your lost youth every time you open the closet doors. You probably spent more on clothes then and you can make a few bucks at a consignment shop and then turn around and see if that same shop has anything you can buy that makes you feel confident.

There are ways to work around financial barriers and still live a full and wonderful life. Trust me. As someone who is recovering from a credit card addiction, I understand what it feels like to be inundated with more bills than income. That brings me to my next "get your shit together" item: money.

Before I say anything, just know that this is a judgment free zone. I've taken trips I shouldn't have, gone to at least a hundred concerts I couldn't afford, and I sometimes spend more on groceries than a 5-person family. I have no business doling out financial advice. However, I've recently made a monumental stride to fix my finances. I took out a personal loan for $35,000 to pay off credit card debt and one small student loan. Sadly, that still leaves me with other student debt but in 5 years, after 60 payments of $870, I will be student loan debt free.

The only problem is, I'm still allowed to spend money on credit cards. There's no law against me going into further debt. So, the goal is to quit spending on any credit cards cold turkey. It has been one of the most difficult things I've ever done, and I haven't been completely successful. For more than a decade, I've relied on credit cards for everything. I am a teacher so, while I make enough money to live, it doesn't always feel that way when I'm shelling out nearly half of my monthly income on debt. I have had to make some choices that I normally wouldn't have to make. I have to skip some nights out at the bar, go to fewer concerts, and keep my shopping to a minimum. It's kind of a bare bones budget at this point. Sometimes I feel sorry for myself, but I just keep running the following banner across my brain space one hundred times a day: IT WILL ALL BE OVER IN 5 YEARS! It's true. If I can work to save my money and stop spending on credit, I will be able to buy a house in five years. That wasn't an option before I got this giant loan.

The point is, learning to get your finances in order is a lot like having a yard sale or cleaning out your car. If you have an end game, a goal you can focus on, it makes everything seem less overwhelming.

One of the final ways to get your shit together is directly related to food and that is to organize your pantry, refrigerator, and freezer. According to a *CNBC* report, as a nation, America wastes around $165 billion in food every year. That is a staggering statistic.

A lot of times, our gut reaction is to eat everything on our plate to stand in solidarity with starving children across the world. Well, leaving a few bites of your loaded baked potato won't solve childhood hunger but a place we can do better is in our own homes. We tend to pile cans and boxes of food in our pantry and freezer and then never see those food items again. Let's say you buy a bag of coconut flour because you need one tablespoon of it for a recipe. Now, five years later, that bag of coconut flour is still staring at you from the back of the pantry.

A strategy to help you eat better and smarter is to clean out those areas of your house. You can take aging non-perishable items (like those weird flours and random cans of vegetables) to a shelter where they can put it to good use. If something is rotten or expired, get rid of it. If you must buy in bulk, organize your freezer and pantry so that you can actually see what you have on deck. This way, you won't buy the same thing 300 times in a row.

A difficult challenge of eating healthy is that buying produce is expensive and if you're the only one eating it, it tends to go bad quickly. A way to remedy at least some of that is buying frozen fruits and vegetables. If you're wanting a salad, only buy exactly what you'll need for a week. Don't buy a whole bag of apples if you're only going to only eat three of them. You will get into a routine eventually and learn to waste less.

Having quick, easy choices available at home that aren't moldy or wrapped in freezer burn will not only make you feel lighter mentally, but you will also be able to make better decisions.

I don't recommend making all of these changes at once. Start by buying a planner and cleaning out your car. Or, just make one small change a week. Break up all of the difficult and overwhelming aspects of your life into categories and start chipping away at what you can. What is the easiest change you can make right now? If you go every day with the constant burden of thinking that you are drowning in every aspect of your life, it's difficult to function. Give yourself a chance and get your shit together.

Extra Fancy & Extra Healthy

Squash Ravioli

Ingredients:

- 1 large yellow squash, sliced
- ½ cup low fat cream cheese (room temperature)
- 4 ounces chopped mushrooms
- 1 tablespoon minced garlic
- ½ cup low fat Alfredo sauce (Buy a jar or make a low-fat Alfredo using low fat milk, low fat cream cheese, garlic, parmesan, and cornstarch to thicken)
- Non-stick cooking spray
- Salt, pepper, garlic powder to taste
- Green onions for garnish

Pro Tip: You can slice the squash with a knife but using a mandoline slicer will result in the long, even slices you're looking for.

Directions:

Using a mandolin slicer, take the squash and vertically slice it with the mandolin so you have long strips. Slice the entire squash and when you're done, lay them all out on a paper towel and add salt, pepper, and garlic powder to both sides.

In a small bowl, combine the cream cheese, minced garlic, and mushrooms. Take two similarly sized strips of squash and cross them (like a lowercase t). In the center where the two pieces meet, add a dollop of the cream cheese and mushroom mixture.

Then, bring up all four sides of the squash, essentially making a pocket. Stick a toothpick in it to hold it together. Heat a skillet that has been sprayed with non-stick spray.

You can use olive oil if you'd like. It does add flavor but also calories so it's your call. You don't *need* it. As the skillet heats up, continue making the "ravioli."

Place them all in a single layer in the skillet and let them cook for 2-3 minutes. At this point, you should be able to remove the toothpick and flip them over to cook a couple more minutes.

Heat your alfredo sauce (I just pop it in the microwave). On a plate, add several of the cooked ravioli.

Drizzle alfredo on top and garnish with green onions.

Cauliflower Fried "Rice"

Ingredients:

- 1 boneless, skinless chicken breast
- 1 bag of cauliflower crumbles (Fresh or frozen)
- 1 teaspoon sesame oil
- 1 tablespoon of light butter spread
- 1 tablespoon teriyaki sauce
- 1 teaspoon soy sauce
- 1 zucchini, diced
- ½ cup chopped mushrooms or other vegetable
- 1 small onion, chopped
- 1 egg
- Salt, pepper, and garlic powder to taste

Directions:

In a sauté pan, add oil and butter and let the pan get hot. Chop the chicken, and let it cook on each side for about 3 minutes.

Now, this is the hard part. Except the egg, dump all the rest of the ingredients into the pan. Cook it through, adding spice and sauce to taste.

Then, form a well in the middle of the pan. Scooch everything to the edge. Drop the egg (after you crack it) in the middle of the pan and basically scramble it. Add a tiny bit of salt to the egg.

If you're a fan of the runny yolk, skip the well, crack an egg on top of the mixture and pop it in the oven so it bakes on top and keeps the yolk. It's up to you.

Zoodle Pad Thai for One

Though I find the term "zoodles" annoying, they are all the rage for a reason! I've been making them for some time and it's because as with anything, eating healthy is largely a mind game. Turning a noodle into a pasta shape doesn't provide the satisfaction of eating a giant bowl of pasta but it does help with the "feel" of eating pasta. What I like to do is lessen the amount of actual pasta I would normally eat and combine it with the zoodles, so I can get the best of both worlds.

Ingredients:

- 1 ounce whole wheat Angel Hair Pasta or Rice Noodles (half of a "normal" serving)
- 1 large zucchini (You'll need some type of zoodle maker. Mine is cheap so it doesn't have to be fancy)
- 1 egg
- 1 tablespoon salted peanuts
- 1 chopped green onion
- 1 teaspoon minced garlic
- 1 teaspoon chili garlic sauce (or more if you like it spicier)
- 1 pinch crushed red pepper
- 1 tablespoon peanut sauce (I use the kind that is not spicy)
- 1 tablespoon soy sauce
- Salt, pepper, garlic powder to taste

Directions:

Bring a pot of water to a boil and add pasta to cook.

While that is in process, wash your zucchini and cut off the end. Use the spiralizer to make zoodles from the entire zucchini.

Add salt, pepper, garlic powder to the zucchini.

When pasta is cooked, drain the water, and add the pasta back to the pot. Throw the zucchini in with the pasta.

Keep the burner on low. The heat from the pasta and the continued cooking will be enough to cook the zucchini. You don't want to pulverize it.

In the pot add the minced garlic, chili garlic sauce, peanut sauce, crushed red pepper and soy sauce. Stir it all together.

In a small skillet, heat it to low-medium heat with non-stick cooking spray. "Fry" an egg, only cooking a couple minutes on either side so the yolk is runny. Add salt and pepper to each side.

Grab a cutting board and chop both the green onions and the peanuts.

Take pasta/zoodle combination and add it to a bowl.

Gently add the fried egg to the top and garnish with peanuts and green onions.

Greek Cucumber Roll Ups

I'm not sure if it's correct that I label anything I put Kalamata Olives on as "Greek" but I don't see myself stopping anytime soon.

Ingredients:

- 1 large cucumber (it would be best to have a mandolin for this and I mean the kitchen tool, not the instrument)
- Hummus
- Kalamata olives
- Reduced Fat Feta Cheese
- Toothpicks (these are not to eat)
- Optional: Sliced deli meat. It would ease right into the recipe nicely.

Directions:

I suppose if you are really skilled with a knife, you could do this or if you aren't, you could make little cucumber sandwiches instead. It would taste the exact same, it just wouldn't feel as fancy.

Run it through a mandolin in long, thin slices. How much you use of each ingredient is up to you. You can add other things like onions or tomatoes if you want.

All you do is spread a thin layer of hummus on the slices, and then sprinkle the olives (I chopped them) and feta on top. Roll them up and stick a toothpick in them. These are a fantastic party alternative for people tired of pigs in blankets.

7

Hangry Angry Beast

My friends and family will think it's funny that I'm trying to encourage people to be Zen because I'm a high-strung dickhead but once again, I'm talking to myself here. Let go of the people and things that make you hostile. Shake off those negative feelings. Scream in the backyard, set something on fire (in a safe and legal environment). Just let it out somehow.

In today's world, we wake up, scroll through our feeds, and are faced with a barrage of terrifying and enraging news. After we read one story after another that feels like a punch to the gut, we are then expected to perform a series of tasks and function in this insane hellscape that is life. Of course, it's difficult to be pleasant all the time.

In addition to the world around us, we also have to deal with our daily lives. Not only do we have to work with a slew of idiots at our jobs, we have to interact with family and friends that drive us nuts.

What I'm saying is that I realize that it's not easy to be nice all the time. I certainly don't maintain a pleasant attitude. I let out these enormous sighs several times a day. There are times when the sighs are brought on by a specific moment, but usually, they come out of nowhere. I will suddenly suck in all the air in the room and then let it out in a long, frustrated breath. Anyone in my presence immediately asks what's wrong. Most of the time, I have no idea why I sighed. It is essentially a habitual form of expression for me at this point.

Not only do I sigh, I can also make a sailor blush with my foul language and can insult your intelligence with one glance. I don't mean to brag but I am kind of an asshole.

Though I'm not what you'd call, "sweet," I do care about people and do whatever I can to support my inner circle. Most of the judgments I impart on others are silent. At my old job, I worked with a few folks who treated our office space like the set of *Mean Girls*. There were head bitches in charge and if you didn't suck their ass on a consistent basis, you were immediately targeted as the enemy. I usually like to fly under the radar, but I found myself at the mercy of someone who was the ultimate decider of popularity.

I spent seven years trying to keep up with the correct ways to behave. It was important to know who I could and couldn't talk to or whose birthday party it was OK to plan and/or attend. I needed to be careful when to indulge on fattening food and when it was time to be serious about weight loss. I never knew if what I was saying was being scrutinized. I later found out that *everything* I said was picked apart and discussed with other people so none of it mattered anyway.

Why did I let someone run my life for that long? I'm not sure. Somewhere along the way, the combination of the fact that we were all forced to work together with my need to just get through every day, I just let it all happen. I hated myself, and the job environment I was in. It was all so petty. What was worse is that even though I knew that I was "above" all of that behavior, my personality shifted, and I became more like the person I hated every day. I sneered at people I didn't even know, and I was a giant ball of negativity.

Once I was set free from the job, I gained heightened awareness of the person I had become, and I knew I didn't want to be that person anymore. Since working there, I've tried to become a more pleasant, positive person who isn't as judgmental as I used to be.

I don't always succeed. I'm the kind of person who cries over menial household tasks. There are moments where I feel like nobody has it worse. It doesn't take me quite as long to gain perspective now.

If we let all of the negative details of life dictate the person we are, we won't be able to focus on being the best people that we can be. Sometimes, life simply doesn't turn out the way we want it to. There are expectations that we have for ourselves, goals that we set, and more often than not, life comes and takes a huge dump on those objectives.

It is then, in our darkest and most disappointing moments when our perseverance is tested. Our biggest tests come after the shitstorm. OK, that didn't work out, what now? Those follow up decisions are what really count.

So, how do we move beyond all of the terrible things clouding our minds? For many, they believe that stress and anxiety are merely weaknesses getting in the way of productivity. People don't make time to take care of their mental health because those who tend to be the most stressed put themselves last. I understand this. How can you possibly have time to take care of yourself when a) everything on that to do list has to get done and b) other people out there have it worse than you so you shouldn't complain.

The problem with this mentality is that when you think that way, you aren't considering the negative effects of leaving your mental health at the bottom of the pile of concerns.

For example, are you getting enough sleep? I know I'm not. I come from a long line of women who don't sleep well, and those genes have been passed on to me. I often have a hard time getting to sleep, but my biggest problem is staying asleep. I toss and turn all night because like many, my brain never shuts off, which means I'm not getting enough rest. According to WebMD, sleep deprivation can cause many alarming effects, including: heart disease, stroke, high blood pressure, diabetes, decreased sex drive, increased likelihood of accidents, depression, anxiety, aging skin, memory loss, weight gain, death, and a myriad of other health issues.

Sleep is critically important and yet so many of us function on around 4 or 5 hours a night. We can't possibly reach our maximum potential and productivity levels if we are not sleeping.

Lack of sleep also emboldens the anxiety and depression you may be feeling. If you are tackling stress every day without getting any rest, your mental health will only worsen. Symptoms of anxiety and depression can come through mentally or physically. When I'm trying to describe my obsessive thoughts, the best way I can manage to do that is to say that it sounds like there are thousands of people living in my brain and they are running around and screaming at the top of their lungs.

There have been times when my anxiety has manifested itself in a physical way. For example, I can sometimes have panic attacks where I can't breathe, and I feel pressure on my chest. Anxiety can cause muscle tension, headaches, sweating, nausea and of course, irritability.

Rather than just accepting your fate as someone who never rests and someone who is miserable all the time, there are treatments that can make you feel better. I have been experiencing obsessive thoughts and anxiety since high school, but I only recently decided to go to a therapist. The biggest factors I had for not going to therapy had to do with money and fear. Therapy isn't cheap. Some companies are fantastic when it comes to mental health and some, not so much. Luckily, I work for a university now and they have a clinic on campus where you can get therapy from a graduate student who has a supervisor with complete training. The cost of these sessions was based on income so luckily, it wasn't too expensive.

What I learned pretty quickly was that it helped to dole out my issues with someone who didn't know me. She didn't have any bias and she gave me some tactics to deal with strained relationships and obsessive thoughts. She did tell me that there is no "cure" for anxiety. That wasn't exactly what I wanted to hear. My general physician prescribed me nerve medication years ago but I'm even anxious about my anxiety pill. I don't want to be dependent, so I rarely take them. My therapist recommended I take them before I know I'll be going into a stressful situation and to combine the pills with other coping mechanisms. Since she said there was no cure, all I can do is consistently work to get better.

So, what are some of those coping mechanisms? Some of the methods didn't work. Meditation isn't something I'm good at, nor is it something I'm willing to practice all that much. I can't center myself enough to allow it to work. The other method I wasn't a fan of was role-play. My therapist, who doesn't know anyone in my family, can't really act as them in a role-playing situation. Every time she would try I would be all, "She would never say that." I think I got on my therapist's nerves because I basically just told her what was going on that week and asked her what to do, but then, when she gave me a method I didn't like to help, I just skipped it.

Everyone is different so some of you may benefit from role-playing and meditation. I'll tell you what has been helpful to me.

First, my therapist told me that one of the main reasons I stay anxious is that I have a tendency to "catastrophize." This is a psychological term that dictionary.com defines as, "to view or talk about (an event or situation) as worse than it actually is, or as if it were a catastrophe." For example, a text from a friend or family member that just says "Ok," when I feel like it could have been a much more thorough text message, may send me into a downward spiral. I will recount every conversation I've ever had with someone to think if I've done something wrong.

If a loved one of mine is traveling, I will imagine their maimed body on the side of the road the entire time they are gone.

For every rejection I receive, my stream of consciousness is a series of insults I hurl at myself and I decide I'll quit writing.

You get the idea.

One of the ways my therapist told me to deal with this was to ask myself a series of questions. They go something like this: What is the likelihood of this happening? Has it happened before? What is the worst-case scenario if this happens? What you are doing when you're asking yourself these types of questions is employing rationale because there is no logic when you are catastrophizing. You simply think the worst is going to happen in every situation.

For me, when I'm doing this, I can't focus on anything else. A perfect example would be my fear of the house burning down. It's not so much the material concern as it is the concern for my dogs. When I leave the house, I sometimes envision my dogs burning to death all because I needed to have a beer. While I know it's not logical for me to never leave the house (thank God my fear isn't that crippling), I take many strides to prevent a house fire. I go around obsessively checking all the candles, the plugs to make sure my flat iron isn't plugged in (even if I haven't used it in weeks), and I make sure the stove isn't on. The weirdest thing I do is that I refuse to leave the dryer running when I leave. If I don't have all of these rituals, I'll think about the dogs the whole time I'm gone.

Recently, a stray puppy entered my life and I have since adopted her. Because she's a puppy, I treat her like an infant baby. I never want to leave her because I feel bad thinking about her crying in her crate while I'm away. What's worse is that she has no way out in a fire. My older dog can leave through the dog door, but not the puppy. When I first got her, I went to the bar but after two drinks, I had to come home. I couldn't stop thinking about the dog being in harm's way. It was an all-consuming fear. I have this ritual when I'm going home that when I hit my neighborhood, I breathe a sigh of relief because I don't see smoke billowing into the sky from my house.

I realize I sound like I need to be admitted somewhere and it's not always bad, but the best way for me to walk myself through those moments is to ask myself that series of questions.

Another method that has worked for me is something called a "worry journal." The concept is that instead of spending my entire day worried, I can allot 10-15 minutes a day to write down my worries. Consolidating the amount of time I spend worrying about everything allows me to fly over obsessive thoughts during the day. For instance, when I'm trying to plan my lessons for the day and I suddenly worry about my crippling mound of student debt, I can say to myself, "Let's worry about that later today." It may seem silly, but it really does help you skip over those concerns that can't be changed in one day. Of course, it's unsettling that I am in such debt, but I can't fix that on a Tuesday when I'm about to teach Modern American Literature.

One of the hokiest solutions she suggested ended up being one of the most beneficial. As I mentioned, I'm not really inclined to meditate. I find it too difficult to completely clear my mind. However, my therapist introduced me to progressive muscle relaxation. There are many times that my anxiety takes on physical symptoms. It's often in the form of chest pains, headaches and difficulty breathing. This method allows you to work through anxiety using your muscles. According to WebMD, the official definition of progressive muscle relaxation is, "a technique that teaches you how to relax your muscles through a two-step process. First, you systematically tense particular muscle groups in your body, such as your neck and shoulders. Next, you release the tension and notice how your muscles feel when you relax them."

It does include slow, deep breaths and attempting to clear your mind like meditation, but having the task of tensing and then releasing the tension of your muscles feels more like you're being proactive. My suggestion on this is to go to YouTube and type in "progressive muscle relaxation," and find a video you like that has a pleasant narration so you can just listen to the video and do what they say. I find the physicality of clenching my fists (and other areas like feet, legs, arms, etc.) tightly and then releasing it, to be very calming.

Finally, as I mentioned, I'm prescribed medication for my anxiety. While I don't want to be dependent on it, I have realized that it's an important solution to rigorous and lengthy panic attacks. I need to be more open to the benefits of the nerve pill. In addition to using it in the moment, I can also use it as a preventative measure. If I know I'm going to a situation where I know there's a high risk of anxiety, then I need to be proactive and take a pill. I find that the best way to cope with anxiety is a combination of medication and calming methods. The important thing to note is that sometimes, you can overcome bouts of panic and other times, it's too overwhelming and that doesn't mean you are weak. Sometimes, it's not something you can simply push through.

For me, the connection between my physical and mental health is strong. I often react to stress and anxiety by eating and self-loathing. First, the self-loathing. When I feel that I am not stronger than my anxiety, it typically turns into depression. For example, one of my primary obsessive thoughts has to do with feeling that I'm going to die from a blood clot that causes me to have a stroke. Pleasant, right? I think this thought a lot at bedtime. I would say that I wake up in a panicked state, feeling I'm about to die, 2-3 times a month. Sometimes, I can calm myself down quickly but others, the feeling is so strong that it causes me to have an intense anxiety attack.

Just the other night, I was sleeping on my stomach and I shot up in the middle of the night gasping for air. Looking back, I think that the combination of my allergies mixed with my big boobs that crowd my chest and lungs at night, were making it difficult to breathe, but when I woke up, I was convinced I was dying. When I think that I'm going to die, and I begin panicking about it, the physical symptoms show up and I can't tell the difference between reality and anxiety. In that moment, my lips began to tingle, there was a significant amount of pressure on my chest, my face felt numb, my head hurt, and I couldn't catch my breath. I was in the throes of a horrific panic attack, but I wasn't sure if it was that, or if I really was dying.

It was so bad that I considered going to the hospital. Because I knew how bad I would feel if I dragged my boyfriend to the emergency room for six hours just to have them tell me it was all in my head, I decided to take a pill and wait. Once I had the calming effect of the pill, I could tell if the physical symptoms I was having was due to panic or an actual illness. It took about an hour, but eventually I was able to realize that it was all anxiety related.

Every time this happens, I immediately head into a downward spiral of shame. I feel like I should be able to ask anxiety to leave as soon as it hits. I relate it directly to weakness. If this is you, I am here to tell you that I understand this feeling of weakness. I also understand that that feeling is bullshit. Having anxiety is something that happens scientifically in the brain. This means that you can no more make anxiety disappear than you can cancer. And, just because anxiety isn't always a terminal illness in the physical sense, doesn't mean that you are weak because you have it. Anxiety and depression are very real issues and you can't just snap your fingers to make it go away. It's important that you know that. All we can do is find effective ways to cope with the hard times our brain can sometimes give us.

In addition to self-loathing, I also react to stress and anxiety by eating. It doesn't take long to find the connection between mental and physical health when we think about the reasons we have poor relationships with food. It is my belief that food is one of the greatest joys in life. It is also something that we need to have a healthy relationship with and that's not always easy. We should eat to sustain life, but also enjoy delicious, new, and fun types of food.

The problem happens when we start eating in a reactionary way. I eat when I'm bored, sad, happy, upset, anxious, mad, tired, etc. When I eat "things I shouldn't," I immediately start berating myself. This is tied to my mental health because my self-esteem is not just low, it's an abysmal wasteland led by a dictator who constantly tells me how dumb, ugly, and fat I am.

Self-esteem issues come from a number of different places, but most people have insecurities in some capacity. For me, it's primarily body issues and insecurities about my teaching and writing abilities. Like anxiety, there isn't a clear-cut way to combat self-esteem problems. We can try to erase the negative thoughts and replace them with positive mantras but if we don't actually believe the nice things we say to ourselves, it's a moot point.

When it comes to dieting, we set up a pass/fail framework that works to further obliterate the way we feel about ourselves. When you say that you are "cheating" on your diet, it means you believe you've been bad. There's this theory that people shouldn't say the word "bad" to their dogs when they yell at them. When you say "bad dog" or yell at them using their name, they will feel like they are completely bad. They will associate their name and who they are with "badness" and they will in turn, feel bad about themselves all the time.

Now, if you're an animal lover like me, you probably don't want to make your dog feel bad about himself or herself. If you're not an animal lover and you think this is dumb, I'm almost done with the analogy. The same idea can apply to the rules we set for ourselves. If we veer from our diet and scold ourselves for being "bad," it's hard to separate the category of food from anything else. So often, when we eat too much or eat something outside the parameters of our diet, we feel guilt and immediately decide that not only are we bad at dieting, we are bad at life in general.

Eating food is one component of your life. The "mistakes" we make with food have no bearing on our careers, abilities, or any other area of our lives. Not only that, eating a big ass piece of cake doesn't mean we are bad at dieting, it means cake is fucking delicious. A healthy relationship with food means that you can eat and enjoy cake without hating yourself for it. The other indication of an unhealthy relationship with food is eating that cake because you are reacting to something. Food shouldn't be a crutch; it should be something you enjoy without emotional impact. Make sense? Yes, it makes sense to me too, but it's hard as shit to get to that point.

Another frustrating facet to having an unhealthy relationship with food is when you are trying to eat healthy and you're looking around and everyone else, no matter what size, is sitting around eating whatever the fuck they want to eat.

I find myself wanting to rain on the parade of those fit looking people who are just inhaling delicious food and be like, "Did you know that has like 100 grams of fat?" I mean, I don't, or at least I hope I don't, but I want to.

If you find yourself irrationally angry at a thin person eating chicken wings, you more than likely don't have the best relationship with food.

The fact is, making healthy choices with food and exercise is a positive thing. However, working on our mental health is critical to success in the area of physical health. Taking care of your body is important because you want to have a long, wonderful, healthy life. However, if we are constantly a ball of stress because we don't want to starve and/or be overweight, it's going to be extremely difficult to live a carefree, happy life. Take my advice and I'll try to work on it too. Let's not believe every choice we make that isn't perfect means that we are failures. It's a dirty lie that your brain is telling you.

Relax. Take a breath. Love who you are! You are wonderful!

Tame the Beast!
(Fun, Belly-Filling Meals)

Ground Chicken Tacos

Sometimes I don't love the consistency of ground turkey. I love turkey on sandwiches and at Thanksgiving, but ground turkey is fickle at best and dries out in no time. The past couple years, I've made ground chicken my go-to protein. It's lean and more agreeable. It's also readily-available at most stores. I use it for almost everything unless I have a horrible craving for red meat.

Ingredients:

- 1 pound ground chicken
- 1 packet or 2-3 tablespoons of taco seasoning mix (Store bought seasoning or make your own. Taco seasoning includes paprika, cumin, chili powder, garlic powder, onion powder, salt, and pepper)
- 1 package of taco size soft tortillas (you can also use crunchy taco shells or big-ass lettuce leaves if you are leaving out carbs)
- 1 onion, chopped
- 1 cup lettuce, chopped
- 1 tomato, chopped
- 1 can refried beans (prepared according to can)

- Shredded cheese (I use low fat and try not to eat all of it before dinner)
- Sour cream, salsa, guacamole, salt, pepper, and garlic powder to taste

Directions:

In a non-stick skillet sprayed with cooking spray, beginning heating the ground chicken. You want to break it up into small pieces and cook it all the way through (which means no pink, y'all).

There's not a lot of fat in the ground chicken so you may want to add a little oil or butter but it's not necessary.

Once the chicken is cooked all the way through, drain any excess grease. Add half cup water to the pan along with the taco seasoning. Let it simmer until the water has cooked off.

Once the meat is cooked, take the tortillas. Smear whatever you like on bottom. My order is beans, guac, and sour cream. Then, I sprinkle on some cheese.

Add chicken and then top with the veggies. I'm not reinventing the wheel here or anything, but I make a damn good chicken taco, and we have taco night a lot at my house. For a quick and easy dinner, it's a no brainer.

Sloppy Chicken Heathers

Ingredients:

- 1 tablespoon low fat butter spread
- 1 tablespoon minced garlic
- ½ yellow onion, chopped
- 1 pound ground chicken
- ½ cup of your favorite BBQ Sauce
- Low fat buns or whatever your preference
- Salt, pepper, garlic powder to taste

Directions:

Heat butter spread in a skillet on medium heat. Sauté chopped onions for 5-6 minutes. Add garlic. Stir a few minutes.

Push onions and garlic to side of the skillet. Add ground chicken after seasoning with salt, pepper, and garlic powder.

Break up the chicken and let it cook all the way through.

Mix chicken, onions, and garlic together.

Take a paper towel to dab up any grease in the pan. Add barbecue sauce.

Mix it all together, and you're done.

Pro Tip: I prefer the taste of BBQ sauce to the tomato-based Sloppy Joe sauce and I don't like peppers so, this is my version. Feel free to sub in Sloppy Joe sauce in yours!

Beer Chili

Chili is hearty and a bowl of it feels like a warm hug. I have played with a number of chili recipes and found that adding beer is my favorite way to add depth of flavor. I like this alone, with tortilla chips and cheese or on top of a hot dog. The best part is, chili is filling and packed with protein. It's a meal all in itself.

Ingredients:

- 1 pound lean ground beef
- 1 pound pork sausage (mild or hot)
- 1 bottle beer (I prefer a brown or amber ale because it adds a richness without being overpowering)
- 2 cloves garlic, minced
- 1 yellow onion, chopped
- 1 tablespoon cumin
- 1 tablespoon oregano
- 2 teaspoons chili powder (more or less depending on spice preference)
- 1 tablespoon smoked Paprika
- 1 regular can black beans
- 1 regular can diced tomatoes
- 1 regular can diced tomatoes with green chilis
- 1 small can tomato paste
- 1 regular can tomato sauce
- 1 cup water
- Salt, pepper, garlic powder to taste

Directions:

In a large stock pot, brown ground beef and pork together on medium heat after seasoning with salt, pepper, and garlic powder (crumbling into small pieces).

When it's cooked through, drain it in the strainer and set aside. Add onion to pan. Let it soften for two-three minutes and then add garlic.

Once the garlic is fragrant, add beef back to pot and add the rest of the ingredients. Stir until combined.

Let the chili come to a boil, turn the heat down and let it simmer for 20 minutes. Serve how you want and enjoy!

8

Get on that Bucket List

Earlier, I argued the importance of getting your shit together financially, but I also believe strongly in having a multitude of experiences. Experiences, whether they are related to travel, or music, or risk-taking, define who we are. They allow us to step outside of our comfort zone and discover new and wonderful things.

In my early 20s, I made a list on my computer I called, "Things to do before I'm 30." Some of my friends who are a bit older than me scoffed when I told them about this list. With condescension, they let me know that while goals are nice, a list like that would never go the way I planned. I realize that sometimes life derails your plans but at 33, I've either accomplished, or come close to accomplishing most of the items on my list.

A lot of the items on the list were related to my financial, physical, and mental wellness. I also had many career and travel goals. Sure, I'm poor, but I'm working to get out of debt in the next five years and I have the job I always wanted to have. Don't let anyone scoff at your dreams. Just because they aren't living their best, most productive life doesn't mean that you have to fall into the same trap. If you have goals, go for them.

Goals don't always have to be about career and money. They can also be goals to travel and do things that scare you. My grandmother, whom I love dearly, has some flaws. Aside from her brash way of telling you how she feels about everything from your hair to weight to life choices, she also is scared to death of living her life. Because of her fears, she's never flown or gone on a large boat or left the continent. If she can't get there in a car, she's not going. She doesn't swim. She would never let me walk around the neighborhood with my male cousins because she thought I'd get abducted. She believes everything she reads. As she's gotten older, her fears have gotten worse. Not too long ago she told me that she basically runs outside to get the mail and runs back just in case someone might try to kill her in a drive-by shooting.

For my Grandma, it just doesn't make sense to risk anything. And, of course, I'm poking fun at her a bit, but I do understand that everyone has fears. I have fears. What I try *not* to do though, is let those fears stop me from experiencing life.

I like to take risks, not only to experience what life has to offer, but to also have the ability to say, "Yes, I did that. It was scary as hell, but I did it." People rarely regret doing something they've been dreaming of doing their whole life.

After college, I was terrified to go to graduate school. I could have put a lot more effort into my high school and college years. I knew that going to grad school would mean that I'd actually have to bust my ass to get through and I wasn't sure I was up to the task.

What if I failed? What if I was the shittiest writer in my class? Of course, I was worried that I wouldn't be good enough. And, I wasn't entirely wrong. I discovered that just because I showed talent in my undergraduate creative writing classes, didn't mean that I was going to impress anyone in my grad school workshop. I also found out that I couldn't write papers as well as I thought I could. But I pressed through. I made the effort to do it and I'm so glad I did.

I felt the same fears when I started teaching and when I started writing my blog and when I started my weight loss journey. I forget sometimes that I've been working my ass off for years, plowing through one goal at a time. And, yes, it can be really scary.

Don't let fear make your decisions for you.

As important as it is to reach your career and life goals, it's also important to make goals that allow you to escape. For me, my greatest escapes happen while watching live music and traveling.

Music is something that can break my heart into a million pieces and then in the next second glue it all back together again. Live music makes that feeling even more intense. I've been in love with going to concerts since I was a child. I'll never forget asking my mom to take me to see Boyz II Men at Memorial Auditorium in Chattanooga, Tennessee in 1995. I was 11 years old and the singer Brandy opened. I had listened to their *II* album at least 100 times. It wasn't necessarily my first concert, as I'd seen country artists and other acts at a music festival called Riverbend, but it's definitely my most distinct early memory of engulfing myself in a live music show.

Since then, I've seen well over 200 bands or artists perform live. I've waded through the sand a few times at Hangout Festival in Gulf Shores, I stood in the driving rain for two hours at Midtown music Festival in Atlanta, I sat on a blanket dozens of times at Riverbend in Chattanooga as a child, stretching my neck trying to see and I've traveled all over the Southeast and scattered places throughout the United States to see concerts.

When I think about the times I've seen Mumford & Sons or Grace Potter, I can take myself back there immediately. I remember the pre-teen like joy I felt dancing at a Taylor Swift concert with my Dad as an adult. I can still feel the unexpected chills that darted all over my body as Shania Twain sang "From this Moment On" in Vegas with my best friend. I can vividly imagine the scenery at Red Rocks in Colorado or the foggy, dark atmosphere at the Starplex Pavillion in Dallas. The point is, if I can afford it, I'm going to find a way to see it.

Music is the ultimate escape. I'm sure I've gotten a sideways glance or two when I've lost myself in the music and randomly start dancing (something I'm terrible at) or worse, crying. Y'all, I've cried at *multiple* concerts.

Perhaps live music doesn't do it for you? If that's you, I don't get it, but I recommend finding something that does exhilarate you and do it as often as you can. My other method of escape is travel. I'll do anything I can to get out of the four walls of my small, but lovely, town.

Dorothy said that there's "no place like home," and I don't disagree. While she did say that, she had a wild, trippy experience that she will never forget. She learned a lot about life over that rainbow. Sure, she learned to appreciate her boring ass farm a bit more and learned not to be clumsy around a pen full of pigs, but she also learned that there's a whole world out there. Outside our tiny little lives exists Technicolor, good and evil and heartbreak. That experience changed her life. Maybe we all need a bit of culture shock from time to time.

I'm not suggesting you Google the best places to find horses that change colors or flying monkeys, but I am saying that if you are someone who never takes a vacation, it's time to get on that. Or, if you are someone who goes to the exact same spot on the beach and eats the exact same "all you can eat fried shrimp" buffet every year, you are missing out on so much.

It's no secret that my parents were poor when I was growing up. I never knew how much my parents sacrificed and how much help they needed to make it feel as if we weren't as poor as we really were. They always saved and did whatever they could to give me elaborate birthday celebrations and a kick ass haul from Santa every year. As I grew older, and my brother came along, they had a bit more and basically, we were the most spoiled lower middle class kids on earth.

One of the primary ways we used what little money we had as a method of escape was through travel. In the beginning, we made our budget work by traveling with our entire extended family. Each year, for several years, we went to St. Augustine, Florida. I haven't been since I was a child, even though I'd like to change that soon, but I remember St. Augustine being a magical place.

We stayed in a no-frills motel. As I've grown up, I've become a bit of a snob when it comes to where I stay. My parameter is always "at least as nice as a Hampton." If you have one or two bad hotel experiences, your standards tend to change. The motel we stayed at in St. Augustine had 70s style furniture and shades of pea green that I remember in a haze. When we were in the hotel at night or there while riding out a thunderstorm, we played cards and watched *Saturday Night Live*. I vividly remember seeing people like Chris Farley and David Spade on the screen.

Maybe I remember it so clearly because I would have never been able to stay up that late at home in Chattanooga and watch something as scandalous as *SNL*. We always played on the beach during the day and got to eat out for dinner at night. There was a delicious German restaurant there with a man that played *Edelweiss* on the accordion. This was a place of escape. Even at a young age, I knew that being here was special. I knew that it was a sacrifice my family was making. In addition to going there every year, my aunt Brenda always took a day of that vacation and took me to a Disney park. There I was, a little girl with a Dorothy Hamill haircut and knock off Nike shoes, getting to see Cinderella's castle, a luxury I could have never experienced without the backbreaking work of my family. I only hope that if I have kids one day, I can give them those things.

Eventually, the family trips to St. Augustine dissipated and the four of us (my mom, dad, and new baby brother) started venturing out on our own. Another yearly vacation tradition we started was heading to the coast of North Carolina. We stayed in a condo that my Dad's cousin owned. I have a lot of fond memories of those trips. The Chesapeake Bay Bridge & Tunnel, giant sand dunes in Kitty Hawk, Ocracoke Island, etc. What I don't remember fondly was the godawful 16 hour drive it took to get there. My brother was a nightmare and a half of a baby, y'all. The little asshole spit up constantly and when he wasn't doing that, he was letting out blood curdling screams. Those trips always had some kind of disaster. My brother broke a table once, we got chased out by hurricanes, and cars broke down. We eventually gave up on that vacation.

In addition to the beach life, we also traveled to other places either through my Dad's job (we went wherever his conferences were), or just vacations that they saved up for. As an adult, I've inherited my parent's love of travel, so whenever I can catch a Southwest deal or cash in some hotel points, I hit the road. At 33 years old, I've been to 29 states and 4 countries and I can't wait to keep going.

On those trips, I've always relished in the food and culture of the area. On top of that, I've taken risks while at many of these locations. In Las Vegas, I rode the X-Scream on top of the Stratosphere, a neon green car that rises you up above the city, points downward, and shoots you forward, so it looks like you are about to plummet to the ground. In New York City, I took my mom on a helicopter tour. The biggest risk there was standing in the frigid wind waiting for our turn.

One of my most memorable experiences happened when my mother, father and I were visiting the Royal Gorge Bridge in Fremont County, Colorado. The gorge itself is breathtaking as you stand on the wooden planks as the Arkansas River rushes below you. My mom and I centered our attention on those thrill seekers riding the zip line across the gorge. The zip line is 1,200 feet above the water. It was clear that we both wanted to do it but that it was going to be scary as shit. The scariest element for me at that time was the weigh in. I didn't want to be anywhere near a weight limit on a tiny plastic seat that flew across a death trap. Eventually we just decided to throw caution to the wind and do it. I'm so glad we did.

We made our way up the long trek to the top where we would be leaving the safety of solid ground. Once we were up there, we paid the outrageous price to risk our life. Then, I saw the scale.

Immediately, I was relieved because instead of numbers, the scale merely had an arrow that either went left for "yes" or right for "no." I'd been eating everything in sight for days so I was nervous but I breathed a sigh of relief when the arrow pointed left. I hopped in the seat and though I was excited, I'd be lying if I didn't admit I was nervous. We were essentially sitting in those harnesses/seats they have for children in grocery carts. Before I knew it, I was given a slight shove above the gorge. Going about 30-40 miles per hour, it's the closest I've ever come to feeling like flying. We were so high, that we flew through a cloud and I could actually feel droplets of rain whipping me in the face.

Fear exists; we just can't let it win.

I could write a whole book on all the traveling I've done but I won't bore you with that. It would be like watching someone's home videos for hours. I guess what I'm saying is, I've never let my weight or my fears or anything else (other than money) stop me from doing what I want to do. Debt sucks but knowing that I've been to the top of the Eiffel Tower, seen where I lived as a baby in Germany, and watched Wicked on Broadway, makes it all totally worth it.

Your escapes, or the items on your bucket lists, don't have to be thrill-seeking adventures. You just need to pencil in time to take care of yourself. Some of my best moments of escape have also been clarifying, quiet moments. Riding a four-wheeler in the middle of a ranch in Wyoming with the Rocky Mountains as a backdrop is one of my single greatest memories of complete peace.

Even just looking out the window of a plane is a humbling experience that makes you realize the smallness of your life in this world.

Don't let fear or money or body issues stop you from doing something that excites you. As long as you can pay your bills, throw the rest behind you and go for it.

Sometimes a Cocktail is a Necessity

David's Sunset

I have to give my late friend David a nod when it comes to cocktails. His obsession was a straight up martini. Since I can't really choke down an actual martini, I often had him make me something "pineapple-y and sweet."

Ingredients:

- 2 ounces light rum (Use coconut for more tropical feel)
- ¾ cup pineapple juice
- Splash Grenadine

Directions:

Shake together pineapple juice and rum. Pour over ice.

Pour a couple tablespoons of grenadine over the top of the drink and watch as it makes a beautiful sunset.

Strawberry Martini

My college years nearly destroyed vodka for me, but I've powered through and it's my primary liquor of choice. While I'm not a fan of a traditional martini, I do love flavored ones and I was inspired to make a strawberry martini at home after I had an icy, delicious Strawberry Fields martini at Bobby Flay's restaurant in Las Vegas. It's actually very simple.

Ingredients:

- 4 fresh strawberries
- 1 ½ ounces Vodka (Basically, a heaping shot)
- 1 tablespoon sugar
- 2 tablespoons water (so, half the shot glass)

Directions:

In the bottom of shaker, muddle the strawberries with the sugar. Break them up and combine them thoroughly with the sugar.

Add ice, vodka, and water to the shaker. Shake together and pour the strained contents into a chilled glass.

Garnish with another strawberry.

Earp Elixir

Even though I've only had one of these in my life, I'm honoring David by including his martini. Try if you dare.

Ingredients:

- Vodka (and good vodka too, none of the cheap stuff)
- Vermouth
- Green olives
- Premium Blue Cheese (David would never have eaten subpar cheese)

Directions

In a shaker, combine vodka and ice. If you have sprayer like he did, you can use that to add one spray of vermouth. Otherwise, add just a small splash. Shake the ingredients together and pour in fancy martini glass. Add two green olives that you have removed the pit from and added blue cheese to a skewer and toss into the glass. Enjoy one or two before you pass out because you're going to be drunk. Bye!

Citrus Sangria

Listen, I've decided that if you have fruit in your cocktails, you are basically losing weight while drinking.

Ingredients:

- 1 bottle red wine (not too sweet)
- Half cup sliced strawberries
- Half cup small pineapple chunks
- One large orange, sliced
- 20 ounces diet lemon/lime soda
- ¼ cup Vodka

Directions:

In a large pitcher, mix all ingredients together. Let it sit in refrigerator to cool for at least 30 minutes. Serve over ice with fruit as an optional garnish.

Blueberry Orange Margarita on the Rocks

*You could blend it up if you want but I'm an "on the rocks" kinda girl

Ingredients:

- 1 ½ ounces silver Tequila
- ½ ounce orange liqueur
- ½ ounce blueberry Vodka
- Juice of one large orange (take some of the peel off first for a garnish)
- 8-10 fresh blueberries
- ½ teaspoon sugar substitute (or a packet if you have it)
- Juice of one lime

Directions:

Take blueberries and sugar substitute and place inside bottom of margarita glass.

Muddle the blueberries gently to incorporate sugar substitute. Do this without completely destroying the blueberries. Leave them mostly whole.

Add ice to the glass. Add the rest of ingredients and stir together.

Dilute with a bit of water if you need it. Add orange peel to the glass as a garnish.

Salt or sugar on rim is optional

9

No Judgment

We live in a world where everyone knows everything, and they will make sure to let you know if you aren't doing life the way you should be. While judgmental people don't discriminate with topic, I've had the most experience with judgment when it comes to weight and health.

When you're overweight, people love to tell you how to shed the pounds. The dynamic of the conversation is rarely one that encourages people to love who they are despite the number on the scale. When I first started losing weight, I was disgusted with the way I looked. My health was poor, so I needed to make changes but, in my mind, I had to start changing my physical appearance in order to remotely have a chance of loving myself or anyone loving me. Those who were closest to me knew that I was trying to change my eating habits.

There are two types of people around you when you are trying to eat healthy. You've got the "Oh, you can have one bite" person. This person, usually a fit person who may have body issues but certainly doesn't know what it feels like to be obese, doesn't understand why you can't just have a bite or two if you are just starting a strict diet. Let me tell you why. I didn't get to the point of needing a special scale by having one or two bites of something. I'm a binge eater. Therefore, having one bite of something isn't really a "thing" that I do. If you know someone who is dieting and trying to have will power, it's really fucking rude to push them into having a bite of something. Stop it.

The other type of person, again, someone who has never been considered a pre-existing condition based on their numeric weight, is what I call the "suggester."

"You should cut carbs."

"Have you ever considered drinking less soda?"

"If you start exercising, I bet you'll drop the weight fast."

Listen, you can be the biggest health and fitness guru around, but it doesn't give you the right to shove your ideas down someone's throat. Make sure that the person you're talking to is open to suggestions. As someone who has been hating her body since childhood, and trying to "fix" the problem, I've tried everything under the sun.

I almost never drink sugary sodas, I've tried cutting carbs and I've been working out like a monster for the better part of a decade.

The exercise judgment infuriates me the most. People assume that I don't exercise just from looking at me. My general physician, who has been my doctor since I was a kid, asks me if I exercise every time I go for a check-up. It enrages me. If I've told him once, I've told him 100 times that I'm getting enough exercise. I'm not just *saying* that I get enough exercise. I really do. In fact, sometimes, I do too much.

It's not only my doctor that is perplexed by my fitness routine, it's people at the gym or the park that see me sweating. I have had dozens of people stop me when I'm running to give me a condescending "good for you." Trainers and those exercising around me are often impressed with my stamina. I've had a trainer show confusion by the fact that I work out as long and as often as I do and gain weight.

Guess what? It's perplexing to me too. In order to maintain, I have to eat what most people would consider a diet. In order to lose, I have to eat way less than that. Exercise plays a role in staying healthy but doesn't really help with my weight loss. It is more than disheartening to steadily gain weight for three years when you exercise every day and eat healthy most of the time. It's soul-crushing. I once read that in order to maintain your weight, you are supposed to eat 11 times your weight in calories. If I did that, I'd probably put on 5-7 pounds in a week.

I am not the only person feeling down or discouraged about weight. Remember that the next time you start lecturing someone about the way you feel they should be "fixing" their body. First, there's a difference in telling someone they look beautiful and saying something like, "Wow, you've lost a ton of weight." The age-old adage, "think before you speak" is an effective way to live your daily life.

I am painfully aware of my size, the way I look and how others see fat people. In every situation in my adult life, I scan whatever room I'm entering to see if I'm the fattest person there. In college, I peeked around the classroom, at work, I'd check every meeting out and, in the gym, with all the fit bodies, I am always looking for someone more like me.

I can't decide if I look for those things to make myself feel better or if I'm looking for comfort and security in someone who gets what it's like to be like me. I am simply a glutton for punishment looking for overweight people in the gym. I mean sure, we exist, but let's be honest, it takes a certain amount of courage to step into a gym full of hot bodies and workout.

It's not easy. I do it every day and each time, I walk in feeling insecure about who I am, not only physically but also as a human being. Truth be told, I'm sure there aren't many that notice but I've never been skinny so I'm not sure.

I imagine that skinny people see me and have one or two thought processes: 1) "Oh my God she needs to be here. I can't believe she let her body get like that. I wonder if she has kids. I could never let that happen to me." Or, 2) AWWWWWWWWW! Good for her!" as if I had been so brave to go to the gym all by myself looking the way I did.

Perhaps the biggest reason I feel like people are looking at me and judging how I dress and what I weigh is because I do it to them. I see someone thin and I'll admit, I'm a hater. I always wonder why I never see skinny people with food stains on their shirts. Do skinny people not drop food? Is there some kind of skinny person clause that prevents them from being clumsy?

I also get infuriated when someone who is no bigger than a size 10 complains about their figure. I want to be like, "I used to be twice your size, get over yourself!" It doesn't help that people don't watch what they say. I have known people to say, "That girl is huge!"

Well, let's do some simple math. If you and I are on a lunch date and you point out another woman that you deem huge, then you take a look at me and realize I may weigh more than the woman you pointed out, try to imagine what I am now thinking about myself.

See how that works? Not only is it rude to refer to anyone as huge, but also, we should all try and make sure to consider the company that we are keeping. The exception to this rule is when you're talking about bitches you hate. If there are bitches out there who have cheated with your boyfriend or talked about you behind your back, feel free to lose yourself and call them whatever you want, fat or not.

The point is, people of all sizes can be clumsy, and people of all sizes also deserve to be respected. We should all remember that body image is developed within a human being by the circumstances around them. We all have the potential to see something disgusting in the mirror. My goal is to try to be a part of a community that lifts each other up rather than breaking each other down. It's hard enough out there already. Even silent judgments need to be quieter.

Every person has their own method of coping with daily life and while we may be asked for advice at times, we should only provide it when someone has requested it. A certain program worked for you? Great. That doesn't mean it's for everyone. Be careful about the way you talk to someone about weight, or how you compliment them. Imagine losing 100 pounds and having someone you work with, who has never once spoken to you before, complimenting you. That screams, "You weren't worth my time before!"

I once had a coworker say, "I can really tell today" when I came in to work during my significant weight loss. She only said it certain days. What the hell was she trying to accomplish? I accepted her "compliments" through gritted teeth but it never sat well with me.

We could all benefit from a certain level of balance when it comes to giving/receiving compliments. I know that most people mean well. It's not all their fault that I resent the fact that I wasn't worthy of compliments until I started losing weight.

The other character trait that people pick up when they are obsessive with diet and exercise (whether it's working or not) is that they talk about dieting and exercise during every waking moment. It is beyond rude to ask someone how many calories their giant burger has as they bite into it. Obsessions about food aren't uncommon but it's not something everyone wants to talk about all the time. If you consistently use the same catchphrases over and over, the people you hang out with are annoyed, and they are probably talking about you behind your back.

Listen, you are beautiful. Right now. You won't begin being beautiful after you lose 5 pounds, 10 pounds, 50 or whatever. You are beautiful RIGHT FUCKING NOW. Physical health is important, but your self-worth should not be connected to a number on the scale. When it comes to eating healthy and exercising, you are in control. Other people may make suggestions but ultimately, you are the decision maker for your body. Just because you are filed in a certain category on an insurance chart doesn't mean you are "bad." Do what you have the power to do. You may never run a marathon or eat grilled chicken, broccoli and rice every day for lunch and that's OK. Take care of your mind and your body. Love yourself. Love others.

Sweets for Your Sweet Tooth

Éclair Cake

Ingredients

- 2- three and a half ounce packages instant vanilla pudding mix (if you're a superhero and feel the need to make your own vanilla pudding then more power to you)
- 1 container whipped cream (It's your call on the real stuff or the oil stuff. I like the oil stuff)
- 3 cups milk
- 1- sixteen ounce package of graham cracker squares
- 1- sixteen ounce package prepared chocolate frosting (again, if you feel the need to make your own, go for it but save yourself the time and the trouble)

Pro Tip: My family uses the cinnamon flavored graham crackers and if you're skeptical about chocolate and cinnamon, I get it but, in this recipe, it works!

Directions:

Grab a medium bowl and with a whisk, mix the whipped cream, milk, and pudding mix.

Take the graham cracker squares (break them in half) and layer them in the bottom of a 13x9 baking pan.

Spread half the mixture on top. Add another layer of graham crackers and lather the rest of that pudding mixture on top. Add one more layer of graham crackers.

Finally, spread the frosting over the top of the whole cake all the way up to the walls of the dish.

If you're not good at spreading frosting like me, you can let it chill for a bit in the refrigerator before you try it.

Also, chilling the whole dish is a must before serving. It allows everything to get gooey and delicious. The longer the better, but at least 3-4 hours. This is a family favorite.

My Brother's Cake Crumble Fruit Cake Thing

This recipe is about as simple and versatile as it gets but it's a real crowd pleaser and my brother loves it. Shout out to my friend Stacey for telling me about it years ago.

Ingredients:

1 box of vanilla cake mix

1 stick butter (personally, I like salted kind for this recipe because it's in contrast with the sweetness)

1 large can pie filling (This works with any flavor so choose your favorite. We've tried with apple filling and multiple berry fillings. All work really well)

Non-stick cooking spray

Directions:

Preheat oven to 350 degrees. In a 9x13 baking dish, spray the bottom with non-stick cooking spray. In a large bowl, melt the stick of butter in the microwave or on top of the stove.

Once it's melted, pour the box of cake mix in with the melted butter and combine until you have gravel sized crumbles of cake. In the baking dish, add the pie filling and spread it out evenly.

Crumble the cake crumbs over the top and bake for 25-30 minutes until brown on top.

Ice Cream Cone Cannoli

Ingredients:

- 1 classic cake-cup style ice cream cone
- ¼ cup low fat Ricotta Cheese (If you don't want to buy a whole tub of ricotta, use low fat cream cheese if you have it on hand and make sure it's room temperature before mixing in other ingredients. Who cares? Break the Rules)
- 1 packet sugar free sweetener
- Small splash vanilla extract
- Heaping tablespoon miniature chocolate chips (give or take however many you want)
- Possible garnishes: chopped pistachios, raspberries, or maybe even rainbow sprinkles

Directions:

For this simple recipe, just mix together ingredients and add them to the cone.

Pro Tip: If you want to get extra hype, melt chocolate and dip the rim of the cone in it for some snazz and extra flavor.

10

"We Accept the Love We Think We Deserve"

Whenever a friend gets all hung up on a shitty guy, I always tell them, "We accept the love we think we deserve." I have no idea if Stephen Chobsky knew the power of this statement when he wrote it in *Perks of Being a Wallflower,* but it has been tattooed in my brain space since the first time I read it.

I don't know if my friends receive this line as a hokey way to make them feel better or if it actually has an impact. The truth is, many people, especially women, never find the love they deserve because they don't feel they are good enough. They don't love themselves enough to believe they could actually be loved in return.

While I provide this friendly advice to many of my friends who doubt their self-worth, I still spend every day questioning the love of my significant other. And before that, I went through a barrage of experiences that proved not only do I not believe I deserve to be treated right, I often punished myself by allowing terrible romantic situations.

I understand that a person can be perfectly happy alone and that a relationship isn't required to be a whole person. Yet, I have found myself seeking love and affection my whole life, often from guys who have no interest in giving it.

I've already mentioned my long-term college relationship with a cheating, manipulative dirt bag but he wasn't my only bad decision.

I always thought that losing weight would "fix me." I thought that once I shed the pounds, I'd feel confident and that I'd find a good-looking, wonderful guy. Well, it worked out that way but not before I put myself through dating hell.

There I was, down 100 pounds, ready to go on the prowl. I always felt invisible before losing weight. To a certain extent, it was true. I wasn't invisible to my family and friends but as a whole, most people are shallow. After the weight was gone, I told myself I was now worthy to be loved. The problem was, I obviously still didn't believe it.

Right as I was at the height of my weight loss, it was time for my ten-year high school reunion. Before losing weight, I wouldn't have dreamed of going to my reunion. I was never a fan of high school and anyone I actually wanted to see, I already saw on a regular basis. I was teased a lot in high school for my weight, so I decided to take my new body, the one that was worth something, to the reunion.

That night was an odd combination of everything I expected, but nothing that I wanted. Because I live in the South, I was one of the only unmarried attendees of the reunion. There were far more single men than women so that fact, compiled with the obvious weight loss allowed me to garner some attention that I was most definitely not used to. I was in a small graduating class of only around 80 people so we all knew each other but still, there were those people in high school I didn't interact with much.

Throughout high school, I had two primary crushes. Both of these crushes were miserable, gut-wrenching examples of unrequited love. I had an opportunity to go home with both of these crushes the night of my high school reunion. I'd love to say that I didn't go home with these guys because I was trying to prove some kind of point. I knew they were shitheads who were only noticing my new figure, but I still relished in the opportunity to finally feel as if they wanted me.

At the end of the night, I was talking with the former crush that I wanted to have a more intimate "reunion" with. He was never mean to me and was still obnoxiously attractive. When the moment came, though, I couldn't do it. It wasn't because I was standing on some kind of moral high ground. I mean, I have a mid-level exciting past but nothing outlandish. The point is, it wasn't because of some southern belle standards that I decided not to go through with it.

There I was, down over 100 pounds, still in control top panties, still disgusted with my body, still uncomfortable and unable to reveal my new body to this person. I knew he'd never see me the same way again. We wouldn't be friends anymore. I'd be the chubby high school girl who came to the reunion with a less chubby figure that he went home with. I didn't want to be that girl. I went home and sobbed into my pillow, hating myself for hating myself. I hated the version of myself that loved the attention and I hated the version of myself that didn't take advantage of it.

That night kind of ignited a series of situations in which I proved I had no respect for myself and that my weight loss hadn't changed my mental status in the least bit. I call these "situations" the "Glamourer," "The Asshole," and "The Irish Guy."

The Glamourer

If you're a fan of the show *True Blood*, you may already know what "glamouring" is. If not, I'd be happy to explain. In the show, a vampire can lock eyes with a human and put them in a hypnotic state just by staring at them. Using this version of mental control, the vampire could get the human to do anything they wanted. Well, after I had my new body, I accidentally ran full-force, smack dab, into the world's most successful glamourer.

He came in for an interview at my job when I was working in the corporate world. I couldn't get a good look at him because, even though I was in the interview, I was at the end of the conference table, parallel to him. Despite the fact that I could only see his profile, I could hear his deep Georgian accent, a total cover up for the kind of person he really was.

When we had a group discussion about who to hire, I was the first to choose him. Those in the room giggled because they knew I was jumping at the chance to finally have an attractive guy my age in the department. Not only that, his voice already had me in love. I hadn't even been punctured by his stupid, perfect, Caribbean-blue eyes.

Turns out, he really was the best guy for the job. He was a super skilled computer nerd, but God really blessed him because based on everything I knew about the looks of an IT guy was shot to shit when I met him.

Even though I was more confident after dropping 115 pounds, it was still beyond my capacity for understanding that a guy like him would have interest in me. Once I was face to face with him, I fell immediately in love. I knew that I would. He is easily a 9 or a 9-1/2 but if I'm being honest, he could have been a 7 and I would have swooned.

I knew he was smart but talking to him, he was also extremely cool. He listened to hip-hop, read books and his Georgia roots oozed off him, causing me to salivate.

Truthfully, there's not much worse in this world than a crush, especially for someone who has only had one crush that wasn't just a miserable example of unrequited love. When this guy spoke to me, he peered into my soul with his eyes. I've never been great at looking at people in the eyes. I guess it must be a trust thing. I often get caught looking at people's foreheads rather than their eyes. With him, he wasn't going to let that happen. He used his eyes as a tool to stick a flag in both my heart and private parts so that he owned me. I was putty in his hands and he knew it.

What's ridiculous is that despite all the flirting he did, it took some very aggressive moves from him before I believed he was actually interested. It didn't help that he had divulged to me that he had a girlfriend on the west coast and that he had failed to mention he'd be leaving in a year to be with her in his interview. I guess once I figured out he had a girlfriend and he'd be leaving, I decided he was off limits. Not only that, I didn't think there was any way the "hot guy" in the office would want anything to do with me. I know. I have awesome self-esteem.

At some point, we transitioned from being work friends to being friends outside of the office. I don't remember the first time we crossed that line, but I was happy we did. Usually it meant that we would grab drinks at a bar with his friends or hang out at his apartment. He was always in seduction mode. He'd look at me for several minutes at a time, make sure our hands touched if he passed me something. I still thought I was insane. I would tell my best friend and she would tell me adamantly that he wanted me, but I couldn't process.

Two separate moments happened prior to the first night we became more than friends that allowed me to finally believe he might be out for more than just a work wife. The first was after we had dinner alone at a barbecue joint. It was awkward and date-like, but I didn't make anything of it until he told me that he and his girlfriend were in an open relationship. Well, I knew he was lying. I knew because he immediately backtracked a bit and said that they just didn't ask each other any questions. Then he went further and made me swear to never tell anyone.

I allowed myself to believe this lie because I knew it meant I could justify anything I did with him. Not too long after that, we saw an impromptu Alabama Shakes show at a dive bar in Tuscaloosa called Egan's. While we were there, he danced behind me and his physical interest in me became clear. I knew it for sure at that point. I was terrified. What was I going to do if he actually pursued me?

Even after that night, I tried to let it go. I tried to play it off like it never happened. I'd known him for months now and I had ignored every advance. I'd become friends with his friends, watched him as he disappeared for several minutes at a time to talk to his girlfriend, and I'll be honest, I'd fallen head over heels in love with him. Avoiding these advances seemed like the easiest way to protect my feelings. I didn't feel confident enough for physical contact and I wasn't ready for him to dump me as soon as he left for the summer.

Well, either he didn't pick up on these insecurities or he didn't care what damage he would do because the night I'd been both dreading and dreaming of finally came. We went out as a group with his friends. We all ate dinner and drank. I never really *ate* around him. I also tried to never drink too much. So, I was merry but not smashed. I wish I had been smashed. He did what he always did. He vanished for about 20 minutes. I knew he must have been talking to his girlfriend. I knew she must have been questioning him, wondering if he was being on his best behavior. I knew he was lying to her, saying that he was just hanging with his friends and nothing more.

He came back in. We were both sitting at the center of the table, facing each other. He started glamouring me. He just stared, and I felt like my skin was separating from my bones. I felt like my eyes were never going to be the same again when he mouthed something at me from across the table.

One thing about me is that I am *super* awkward, so I never pick up on verbal or subtle cues. I can never hear anything anyone is saying and I'm always available to screw up a punch line. So, of course, I didn't hear what he was saying. It took him several minutes to get the message across. When I did finally understand he was trying to take our relationship to the next level, I giggled then ran away to the bathroom. I called a friend of mine. I think I was looking for permission to be with him. I knew he had a girlfriend and I knew it would only end in a disaster, but I wanted someone, anyone to tell me to go for it. I should have called someone else. My friend told me to put myself in the shoes of the girlfriend. I don't know why I called anyone because I knew, at the end of the day, that I would do whatever he wanted.

169

We went to another bar and he asked to talk to me. I followed him, the way a puppy follows her person around the house when they are cleaning. We went out the back door of the bar, down a step and stood in the dark alley where the lingering smell of bar trash filtered into my nose.

Before I could say anything, he kissed me. I'd like to say that sparks flew out either sides of our mouths but instead, we both faced our heads the same way and our front teeth clanked together. We tried a second kiss. The second one felt more like what I had imagined. I could feel warmth in my cheeks and chest. My pulse quickened. I was excited and devastated at the same time. I was so fucking fucked.

Once we pulled apart and I couldn't taste the cheap beer in his mouth anymore he said, "I've been wanting to do that forever." I feigned some mild concern about his girlfriend. He remained silent on the subject.

Physical contact with the "glamourer" was an overwhelmingly unenjoyable experience at first. The fact was that even though I'd lost 115 pounds, I still felt huge. I couldn't figure out how someone with both a nice body and face could want me. Anytime I was around him, I expected it to end any second. I also sucked in to an unnatural point and attempted cover up my belly and butt if I felt like they were exposed in any way. I wore a lot of flowy dresses and shirts.

Once we passed the friendship label, I was not confident about the future. It would be awkward at work. Our friendship was over.

Well, I was wrong. He certainly made it clear that the boundaries of our relationship were strictly on a friends-with-benefits level and that I had to keep it quiet, but it was also clear that he wanted to continue what he started until he left. I look back now, and I am sickened by the fact that even though I knew he would never give up his trip out west with his cute girlfriend for me, I still went willingly into a several-month relationship with him. It never once occurred to me to tell him no. How could I? I was receiving such a gift.

Barf. My self-hatred causes even more self-hatred.

The relationship ended exactly as I knew it would. I'd grown totally attached to him. I was in love. He and I had very little in common when it came to politics and religion, but I morphed myself into a person I had hoped he could fall for. It was all for nothing. I said goodbye to him. My friends comforted me, but I was broken. In my mind, the weight loss hadn't worked. I did what I was supposed to do, and I still didn't end up with the guy. I've since gotten better at realizing my self-worth isn't connected to the love of a man...or at least, it shouldn't be but damn, it wasn't a lesson I was ready to learn.

One day, if I have children, and they ask me about my pre-marital relationships, I feel like I will tell them that their aging, chubby mom loves their dad, but she once had the attention of the hot guy. I hate it, but I look upon that time as both a victory lap and an embarrassing failure.

The Asshole

It would be nice if I learned my lesson from the Glamourer. Wouldn't it be lovely if I could tell you that I never chose another man who wasn't good enough for me or treated me like shit? Welp,

I can't tell you that. In fact, I had the shortest turnover ever for picking a giant bag of dicks to pine after.

When the Glamourer left, I needed to get over him quick. God forbid I attempt to salvage any dignity and spend some time reflecting on my actions or need to be loved by a guy. Before the wheels could leave the ground of the Glamourer's plane (and truthfully it was a bit before that), I jumped head first into the online dating world.

As a general rule, I discovered that if you use an app that's free, most of the people just want to hook up. If you pay for the app, you get a less sketchy pool of guys to choose from. Ultimately, they still want to hook up but hey, at least they'll take you to dinner first.

I had my fair share of experiences from online dating. Mostly I found it overwhelming. I'm not bragging here (seriously, I'm not. It happens to everyone) but I had a ton of running conversations in which I was trying to maintain a unique and flirty rapport. It was exhausting.

Once I narrowed it down, I had a few dates. Being a left wing, alcohol loving, career-oriented woman in the South makes it difficult to find someone you can do life with without killing each other. Most of the men I found had fundamental differences I couldn't deal with. I don't mind disagreeing with someone on politics but if you hate gay people, we aren't ever going to make it.

The online dating game descended quickly into an exercise with two outcomes. 1) Long talks with someone you connect with and then find out they are awful in person. I don't mean looks necessarily, but chemistry is chemistry, and when you meet someone, and your first instinct is to run away, you aren't going to be a good match. I met a guy who was witty in an online forum but in person brought tears to my eyes because he was so boring. Then there was the guy who I loved talking to and then suggested we Facetime. When I finally got him on the phone, he sounded like Screech from *Saved by the Bell* and I could see a Samurai Sword hanging on the wall in the background.

I'm not a shallow person, though it sounds like I am. I was trying to be somewhat picky. I had just been in a long-term fling with a guy who was both smart *and* cool. I mean, he was awful to his girlfriend (as was I) but hot so it was OK. Truth be told, I probably could have been less snobby then, especially since I ended up sticking with the worst possible choice of online date. 2) There is a guy who wants sex and nothing else. Online dating is not glamorous or for the weak. It's an exhausting venture.

I won't bore you with all the details of my online dating life. If you've ever done it, you know. I think that online dating is great in a large city. Smaller towns in Alabama are very hit or miss. I joined because I wanted to "get out there" and "date around." Mostly it's just a series of let downs after you've decided you've found your soul mate after one "Hi" and a smiley face on a phone app.

One person I did find seemed perfect. He was a bearded guy who had graduated from law school (though he had failed the bar like 7 times) and he loved to cook. He used correct grammar, wanted to show me all kinds of new music when we talked, shared similar political views and he was funny. We chatted quite a bit. He lived about 45 minutes from me. He was clear that he didn't want a relationship. He was trying to get over the love of his life so only wanted something casual.

Because I don't think I deserve better than someone who only wants to use me, I decided to give it a shot. He insisted I come to him of course. The first night we were together, it was fun. It felt casual, but it also felt like I could definitely change his mind. He would forget all about whatshername. I didn't even consider the possibility that I may not need to be with him in the long run. I just went for it.

I learned early on that this guy was a bit off. He was an amazing cook. I'll give him that. He made these tender, delicious meatballs that I adored. One night, he made a soup. It had tons of vegetables that he was chopping. He looked up from his professional knife work show to look at me and cut his finger. He never forgave me for that. The way he spoke to me after changed.

Once I came over and he told me that my mascara made me look like a whore. He was mean and tried insisting on doing things I didn't want to do. He told me about sick things he dreamed about. He was not a good person. Keep in mind, this was over a period of several months and I kept going back. He told me nearly every time that we would never be together.

I guess in some ways I was punishing myself for something. Maybe I was punishing myself for being a part of a guy cheating on his girlfriend. Maybe I was punishing myself for not being skinny and pretty enough for that guy to love me. Maybe I felt I was just getting what I deserved for not hitting my goal weight.

He came to my house once during our entire encounter. I was too ashamed to tell anyone in my family what I was doing. I would have never given them the details of our physical encounters, but I tell them everything. Under normal circumstances, I would have told them about a guy I was seeing but I couldn't. I was too repulsed by my actions to admit that I was allowing myself to be bullied by some loser who used his parents' money to get by and couldn't be a real lawyer because he wasn't as smart as he thought he was.

Thankfully he ended it for me. He acted like he was a martyr when he did it too. He knew he could never be with me, so he ended it. What's sad is that I told him I could handle it. I could still see him and not expect anything, but it was over. Occasionally he still contacts me. Mostly he asked to see my boobs or my friend's boobs. She also went on a date with him before I did. That's another thing about online dating in the South…there's a lot of crossover. She was smart enough to never let it get anywhere. I wish had been.

The Irish Guy

Getting over the Asshole wasn't as difficult as moving past the Glamourer. I was upset of course but I was also numb. I was climbing an uphill battle keeping off the weight I'd lost. All I wanted to do was eat and drink. I hated myself because I hadn't reached my goal weight and I could barely maintain the success I'd had. I have never once let myself be proud of my accomplishments for more than one single fucking second.

When I met the Irish Guy, I had stopped online dating. I was having fun, or at least trying to, and I was just flirting when the opportunity presented itself. Other than that, I was trying not to focus on finding anyone too much.

That didn't last long. In addition to being "The Irish Guy," the next guy had many other insensitive monikers I won't mention here, but he was definitely another example of my inherent need to make the wrong choice in guys during this time in my life.

The night I met Mr. Irish, I was at a bar with my best friend. We were sitting at the bar when I noticed him on my left. I was

175

already being nosy, catching glimpses at his face and trying to see who was texting him and what they were saying. He was wearing a hat, t-shirt, and jeans. He was slender, but I couldn't tell just how slender until later. He had the perfect length of stubble on his face. The hairs were all different shades of red, brown, and white.

I don't usually just step out and flirt with guys. I was feeling particularly frisky this night though and when the Irish Guy closed his tab and started to get up from his bar stool I said, "Oh, are you leaving?" I gave my best "pouty lip" and his eyes lit up and he said, "No, no I'm not leaving." He opened his tab back up and started buying me drinks. In the history of my adult life, this tactic (or any tactic for that matter) had never worked for me. I was shocked but quite pleased with myself.

That night, we talked for hours and then he went to his house and I went to mine. When I got home I was still reeling. He texted a sweet message that same night. He was from Ireland originally and had moved to America permanently after meeting his wife, but they got a divorce soon after. He didn't give me many details on this and of course, I didn't bother to focus on it much. His accent made me swoon and before I knew it, we'd set up a date.

I was far too excited to go on an actual date. It didn't happen often and after the two previous disasters, I was finally going out with someone who wanted to actually be in public with me in a romantic capacity.

We got along great. He was sweet and funny and open minded. He thought I was beautiful, or at least he said it. Sadly, I felt more insecure than ever. I was still stuck in a plateau with my weight and the Irish guy had a 28 inch waist. 28.

After we spent a couple perfect weeks of dating, it all came crashing to a halt when he told me that years before that he had been diagnosed with bipolar disorder. He'd spent time in a hospital because of it and, due to the consequences of the disease, he was 100% certain that he would never marry again or have children.

When he said all of this, I couldn't process it at first. I mean, I have anxiety but thankfully, it's never been crippling. I didn't understand how serious his disease was. When I tried to discuss a scenario with him in which he would change his mind, he was emphatic. I was a tire that had just been deflated, no, mutilated by a butcher knife. I had gashes in my chest and all the life was torn from me. I know it sounds dramatic, but I thought I'd finally faced enough man trauma. What's funny is that before he told me he wouldn't get married or have kids, I wasn't even sure those were things that I wanted.

Once again, instead of ending the relationship that would only end up in sorrow, I stayed in it. I told him I was fine with it and we still saw each other. Over time, his bipolar disorder revealed itself like the obvious twists in a Lifetime movie. It isn't just about mood swings. It's about the inability to achieve happiness without a significant measure of medication and brutally difficult work. I became attached in a way I didn't understand. I wanted him to be something he couldn't.

I wanted him to come out with me and my friends and not tremble with fear. I wanted him to meet my parents. I wanted him to not text 50 times in a row when I didn't respond the "appropriate" way. I wanted to not get a phone call in the middle of the night that he had tried to kill himself by getting drunk and almost driving off a bridge. He was and is a wonderful man, but it was a toxic relationship in which he hated himself for not being able to accommodate my needs and a relationship in which I could never be happy. Even my doctor, who always obnoxiously checks in on my love life, told me to run as fast and as far as I could from him. He said if I didn't break up with the Irish guy, I'd be in for a "lifetime full of misery."

I found myself trying to detach from him. I ignored him more and more. I believe that part of me loved him, but I knew it was a relationship I couldn't maintain. It wasn't until I met my current boyfriend that I cut myself off completely from terrible relationship choices.

Finally, I Catch a Love Break

Sometimes I wonder what shitty relationship I'd be in if I'd never met my current boyfriend, Ian. I was still trying to get past the Irish guy. I was a lonely, hot mess. I thought about my body and all of its imperfections constantly and blamed my body a lot for my bad luck with guys. I realize it could have been worse. I also realize I had other things, like my career, to think about but the blows to my self-esteem felt like the only thing that mattered.

One night, I had gone with a group of friends to play trivia at a local bar. After trivia was over, I didn't feel ready to go home. None of the people I was with wanted to go out, so I went alone to my favorite bar. I sat in the booth by myself and started looking at my phone. The bar was dead, which is weird because it was a Thursday night. The bouncer came by, made a few inappropriate comments and then it was just me again.

A few minutes later, I look up to find a guy sitting down across from me with a sweet smile on his face. As he plopped down on the disgusting, old booths, he just said, "Hi." To be honest, I was annoyed at first. I just wanted to be left alone. At first glance, Ian was not anyone I would have typically sought after. He had a Grateful Dead shirt on, ratty jeans, a pair of slip on shoes that were on their last leg and the worst part, a long, curly ponytail that hung down the middle of his back.

When he spoke, though, all I saw were his deep blue eyes, surrounded by the most perfect crow's feet. We started talking and we haven't looked back since. Ian is a man-child. Look, I know it seems harsh but it's true. He'd admit it. When I first met him, he worked at a sandwich shop and played drums occasionally. Since we started dating, he's become a full time drummer, and though he's very talented, it's not exactly a ton of money. He sleeps until the afternoon and he drinks too much. He's also the best thing that's ever happened to me.

Ian loves me for who I am, and he makes sure that I know it. He's the sweetest, most accommodating person on earth and there are many, many days that I believe I don't deserve him.

Since we've been together, I have gained almost half my weight back. It's taken me 3 years, but it keeps coming back on. Not a day goes by that I don't think he will leave me. He has no tolerance for my sad-sack shit self-esteem routine. He repeatedly tells me I'm beautiful and talks about how lucky he is.

I'd love to get some of this weight off, but Ian has taught me what real love is. He would never ask me to keep quiet about our relationship. He would never base our love on what I weighed or looked like.

Bad things can always happen in relationships. If I had to guess, I'd say that Ian and I will end up together. However, I'm not naïve enough to think that nothing could ever go wrong. If for some reason we ever part, he will have shown me that I don't have to accept the love I think I deserve. I can wait for someone who treats me like a human being, like someone who deserves the best, kindest type of love.

Nobody is perfect, but I deserve the kind of love that Ian gives me, even if I don't believe it sometimes. You deserve it too. I met Ian when I was almost 30 years old. He was so worth the wait and so worth all the terrible people I was with before. I don't believe you need a partner to be happy. However, I'm happy to have him by my side.

If you don't have this, be patient. Love who you are and don't accept the first relationship that comes your way because you're lonely. Loneliness can happen even when you're in a relationship.

If you are with someone who makes you feel bad about who you are, please, please get out of that relationship. You are so much better than that. Be important enough to yourself to *not* accept the love you think you deserve. Accept only the love of your wildest dreams. Accept love that grosses people out. Accept the love that makes you corny as shit.

Love Yourself, Love Snacks!

Goat Cheese Crostini

You can't have happy hour without proper snacks, or nosh as it's called in certain circles. This recipe is also one of David's!

Ingredients:

- Crostini bread
- *You can slice pieces of a baguette yourself but usually the grocery store has pre-cut crostini in a bag near the bakery. I would do that. It's much easier.
- Creamy Goat Cheese (Or regular cream cheese)
- Sun-dried tomatoes
- Olive oil
- Salt, cracked black pepper

Directions:

Pre-heat the oven to 350 degrees. Spread the crostini in an even layer on a cookie sheet that has been lined with parchment paper. Drizzle olive oil over each piece of bread. Take a knife and spread goat cheese on each piece of bread. Then, top each one off with a few sun-dried tomatoes.

Pop them in the oven for 5-10 minutes depending on how crispy you want them.

181

Shame Free Taco Dip

My friend David was a sophisticated host. Me, I'm a touch more simple. One of my favorite foods in the world is a chip and dip situation. I love tortilla chips and salsa, pita chips and hummus, crackers, and cheese dip. I love anything that requires one edible thing to be dipped into another edible thing and then eaten. I've tried a few dips that cut calories and this one tastes delicious. My problem is that when I know there are less calories, I somehow decide that's reason enough to eat half the pan.

Ingredients:

- 8 ounces low fat cream cheese
- 8 ounces low fat sour cream
- 1 small jar salsa
- 1 packet taco seasoning
- Baked tortilla chips
- Optional: lettuce, black olives, shredded cheese, fresh tomatoes, jalapeños, etc.

Directions:

Beat all ingredients together (other than chips) in a large bowl with a mixer.

Once all ingredients are combined, you can stop there. Or, to make it even more delicious, add shredded cheese, fresh lettuce, and black olives.

You could add fresh tomatoes too if you're into that kind of thing.

Spicy Poppers

Ingredients:

- 4 jalapeños
- 4 slices turkey bacon
- 1-eight ounce package low fat cream cheese
- ½ cup shredded low fat Cheddar
- 1 cup Panko bread crumbs (you won't use the whole thing)
- 4 egg whites (You could also use egg white substitute)

Pro-Tip: Use gloves when cutting the jalapeños, or make sure to wash your hands a billion times and not rub your eyes. That is NOT an easy flavor to get off your hands.

Directions:

Pre-Heat oven to 375 degrees and line a cookie sheet with parchment paper. You will want to have cooked the turkey bacon before starting the preparation. Lots of people wrap their poppers in bacon but I find this to be more trouble than it's worth and I also feel like I never get the texture I want. So, I cook it and add it into the mixture.

While the oven is heating, and the bacon is cooking, combine one 8 ounce package of cream cheese and half a cup of shredded cheese. You can make as much of this as you want so just keep that in mind as you increase/decrease based on the amount of servings you need.

It's best if the cream cheese is at room temperature. You can use a blender, but a fork works just fine. Cut the jalapeño slices in half (vertically). Remove the seeds and membranes with a spoon.

Chop the turkey bacon into small pieces and fold into the cheese mixture.

Take a spoon and evenly distribute the cream cheese concoction into each jalapeño half.

Now, put the egg whites in one bowl and the panko crumbs in the other.

Dunk each jalapeño in the egg whites and then cover in panko crumbs. Line them on the cookie sheet and bake them for 15-20 minutes until the panko is golden brown.

I recommend letting them cool a couple minutes as the cheese will be hot, but you don't want to wait too long because they are most definitely not as good cold. These are the perfect appetizer for a party!

Cuban Quesadillas

Warning: I have a full understanding that Cuban sandwiches have pickles. Please don't feel the need to correct this recipe. I hate pickles. Feel free to add relish or pickles to yours but you won't find them in this recipe.

Ingredients:

- Low carb tortilla
- Sliced deli ham
- ¼ cup cooked pulled pork (This is optional. When you are whipping up a quick lunch, you may not have time to whip up pulled pork. It tastes great without it but if you have leftover pulled pork, it's perfect. Also, you can buy pre-made fully cooked barbecue pork in the grocery store now and that would work well too.)
- 1 tablespoon Dijon mustard
- 2 slices Ultra-thin Swiss Cheese
- Non-stick cooking spray

Directions:

Spray a non-stick pan with cooking spray and bring it to medium-high heat. Once the pan is hot, spread the Dijon mustard on one side of the tortilla then place it in the pan with the other side down.

Let the tortilla heat up a bit and add cheese, ham, and pork to one half of the tortilla.

185

Bring the other half up to make a quesadilla. Let it cook around 2-3 minutes and then flip over.

Essentially the goal is to not burn the tortilla, make sure all the ingredients are warm and that the cheese is melted.

This salty treat makes for a breezy island-like lunch. Go ahead and add a splash of rum to the Diet Coke you have with it. You earned it!

11

Perfection Does Not Exist

My Dad often jests that he's perfect. I love my Dad and all, but he's not. The shitty part about life is that perfection isn't something that can be reached, but we spend so much time trying to achieve it that we waste our whole life away.

My theory is that the way we view perfection is not only flawed, but also dangerous. We place perfection in categories. I need to be perfect on my diet. I need to reach perfection with exercise. I need to be perfect at my job. That's an overwhelming amount of pressure that we place on ourselves. I suppose there's a chance we could find perfection in one or two categories though I feel like it's unlikely.

When we think about mental and physical health, we are often deterred by the fact that we aren't perfect and because of that, we give up attempts to get healthy. When we feel like a repeated failure, we chip away at our confidence with each attempt. How sad is that? Every single week, if I feel like a monumental loser and then have to find momentum to try and become a new, non-failure person each Monday, it becomes an exhausting process.

Imagine if we realized that a) we are awesome and need to understand that our ideas of perfection are generated by arbitrary standards of society and b) perfection is a farce and we need to give ourselves a fucking break. How amazing would that feel?

What I've learned over the years is that perfection doesn't exist when it comes to food or exercise. First of all, for me at least, eating and drinking and being merry is one of the greatest joys in life. I have shared so many food-related memories with the people I love the most. When we analyze every bite that goes into our mouth and berate ourselves for every calorie, we pee all over the joy of food.

I'm not arguing that you should eat what you want when you want all the time. The other extreme of never indulging your cravings is to binge eat. Binge eating isn't enjoying food. It's a coping mechanism.

When it comes to food, do what works for you. I like having a structured plan to follow but I also enjoy copious amounts of beer, cheese, and carbohydrates. The goal is to find a balance in between those two worlds.

It really isn't fair for me to make suggestions about food. I'm a hot mess 99% of the time. I eat well one week and stick to a rigid plan and then the next week it's a free-for-all. I'm ordering pizza, eating Mexican food until I puke and drinking all night. I hate myself so much as a result of this behavior that I eat well the next week. Then, I'm so proud of myself I think I deserve another week of eating everything I see. The reason this happens is because I can't accept that it's OK that I'm not perfect. I can't believe that I find myself in the throes of failure this much. I need to stop. Let's all stop.

One place where I tend to excel is my dedication to exercise. I think the reason I'm so committed to working out at least 5 times a week is because of the deeply rooted fear I have of gaining weight. Despite my consistent exercise regimen and eating well most of the time, I've still gained over half of my weight back, so I often find myself feeling dejected about that as well.

Either way, I have found exercise to be one of the most important elements in my life. Let me say this: I hate it. I have always and will always hate exercising. I hate thinking about needing to work out. I hate putting on workout clothes. I hate the action of exercise and I hate feeling sore after. Some people swear that after a few weeks, you'll start to love exercise. Those people are sent here by Satan to make you feel bad about yourself. Exercising sucks ass. Having said that, I crave it. I need it. It makes me feel accomplished when I feel like a failure in so many other areas.

I don't want to talk about exercise in a way that implies I think there's something wrong with you if you *don't* work out. I want to make it clear: I'm not judging. I'm also aware that there are different abilities within each body. If you aren't able to do certain activities due to a physical or mental limitation, then by all means, don't do it. Ask your doctor what you can do to challenge yourself without getting hurt. However, I am an advocate of movement if possible. I believe exercise is critical and I believe it's a natural booster for mental health (though I am a firm believer in therapy and medication).

Even though I strongly advocate exercise, I'm not good at it. I have never and will never be an athlete. I have experienced discomfort and humiliation when movement is involved on many occasions. I've decided to share some of those stories with you.

The Foam Pit

One of the most embarrassing nights of my life happened at a friend's 30th birthday where I suffered two mortifying situations. Before there was a fall, there was a foam pit. A woman I used to work with was turning 30 and wanted to have a party reliving her childhood so she had it at a place in Tuscaloosa called Tumbling Tides. This was a place that kids could go learn gymnastics. There was a trampoline, uneven bars, huge blue mats, and a giant foam pit. I guess the purpose of the foam pit is to jump from the trampoline and learn leaps and flips without fear because you are landing in about 10 feet of foam blocks.

I was at my heaviest weight at the time. I was wearing white sweatpants. I'm not proud of that. Those can't be good for anyone. Everyone was having a blast and I was more of a casual observer than anything. This woman had a lot of thin friends. By that I mean that they were *all* thin. One by one, I saw thin women less than half my size leaping into the foam pit and then using a rope swing they used to casually pull themselves out like it was the easiest thing they had ever done.

My friend turned to me and suggested that I try it. "No, I think I'll just let y'all have fun." I was already feeling enormous and there were video cameras around. It just seemed like it would end badly. I've always loved trying new things. I try not to let my weight stop me from having fun. Sometimes, it's unavoidable though. I stood there a few more minutes watching everyone exit the pit with ease. "It's so much fun! Just jump in, make your way to the side and use the rope to pull you up." Against my better judgment, my arm was twisted enough to try it. I regret very few things in life but not trusting my instinct with the foam pit is something I wish I could take back.

I stood at the beginning of the trampoline and walked quickly toward the pit. This was as close as I could get to a running start. I reached the jump off point and pushed off with my right foot. Since I couldn't do anything fancy, I stuck both feet together and toes pointed down, landed deep into the foam pit. I could hear laughing and clapping from above but the only thing I could see was hundreds of blue, foam blocks. *Shit. I hate myself,* I thought.

I couldn't believe I had given in to this stupid activity. I pushed my arms forward and reached them high and began swimming. All I knew to do was swim as if I was in water and not a pit filled with foam pieces, meant for gymnastics practice. I began a climbing motion with my hands, inching my way slowly to the surface. My head finally emerged above the foam. I was hoping I had landed closer to the rope and edge, so I could make a quicker escape, but no, I was directly in the middle of the pit.

I looked to my friend, feeling hopeless. She encouraged me to make my way to the rope. I did that. It took a few minutes, but I was able to reach it. In my entire life, I had never been able to pull myself up to do anything. I'm not sure what gave me the idea that I'd suddenly be able to have pull-up strength and drag myself out using this rope, but I tried. I placed both of my chubby hands on the rope and with all my might started pulling. Was someone holding my feet down? It felt that way. I couldn't move. My hands and arms got sore from all my attempts and it didn't take long to realize that the rope plan of action was out, and I needed a plan B.

Looking again for guidance, I was then instructed to make my way to the edge of the pit, so I could just climb over the side to get out. The problem with the pit is that its depth is taller than you are and there are no handles or grips or ladders to help you out. If they wanted fat, out of shape people in the pit, it was poor planning on their part. I made it to the side, but the edge came up to my neck so once again, I was attempting to rely on my arm strength to get me out of there. By this point I was exhausted and it just wasn't going to happen. I tried climbing, running, and pushing but nothing brought me closer.

It was time to bring in some reinforcements. I had been in the pit at least 10 minutes at this point and it was just getting sad. The worst part was that I knew cameras were still rolling. I'm sure it was all in good fun, but I felt like I was on a reality TV show called, "Fat People in Embarrassing Situations." Three men came over to pull me out. I had one man on my right arm and two on my left and after they devised an organized, counting scheme, they were able to heave me to the side of the pit. I rolled over, exhausted, and unable to get up for about a minute. The most disturbing part was that the laughing had stopped and turned to pity. This was my nightmare. I know people have real issues in this world, but this foam pit moment haunts me to the core. It happened almost a decade ago and I still think about it fairly consistently.

Spin

Walking up the stairs to Reese-Phifer Hall at the University of Alabama, I must have looked like I was riding an imaginary horse, both feet spread wide, awkwardness as I climbed each one. I knew that it hurt to walk but I wasn't aware my outward appearance would be so noticeable to others. I was on the debate team and when I got to what we called the "squad room," one of my teammates asked me if I was OK because they spotted me walking into the building and it looked like I was in severe pain. Well, in many ways, I guess I was OK but at the center of who I am as a person, I was not OK. You see, the night before I had just taken my very first spin class.

I have been a part of a few gyms in my life and nearly all of them offered some type of spin class. In college, I was experimenting with different exercises and decided to try one. I always heard that spin burns hundreds of calories because you're working all different types of muscles.

For those that don't know, spin is essentially an aerobics class that takes place on a stationary bicycle. Classes are about an hour and they have an instructor who takes the class through different speeds and resistances while following the beat of several assorted songs.

The first time I tried spin, I wasn't at my heaviest but getting close. I hadn't ridden a bike since childhood and though I had been exercising a bit, I would not say I was in shape. Because of my weight and heredity, I was most nervous about hurting my knees, but I was hoping since I would be sitting, it wouldn't be bad.

I went to my first spin class alone. Walking into the room, the entire place was dark, lit only by glowing equipment and clothing from the black light at the top of the room. Even though I found that a bit strange, I felt comforted by the fact that I could go to the back and stay under the radar. I chose a bike and hopped on.

Immediately, my eyes widened in shock as a sharp pain attacked my vagina. I looked around to see if anyone else was experiencing this torture to their nether region. Some of the participants were casually spinning as a warm-up and others were adjusting their seats.

When I noticed the instructor and several people moving knobs and adjusting their seat height, I hopped off and followed suit. Surely the horrific and awkward pain could be solved with the correct measurements on my bike. I didn't really know what I was doing, and nobody was reaching out to help me. I was also too shy to ask anyone because when I was that overweight, I preferred remaining as invisible as possible.

I fiddled with the knobs and moved the seat up a couple notches. It was time for class to start so as the instructor turned on the fans and closed the doors, I climbed back onto the seat.

If possible, the situation had worsened. I was in excruciating pain. I looked to my right and a fit woman my age was actually smiling. She was pushing the pedals and appeared happy. Her ponytail was so high it looked like she was being lifted off the seat by an invisible rope. I glanced to my left and there was a man, spinning along. *A man can do this?* I thought. If this seat was mauling my vagina, I could only imagine what it was doing to his balls.

I looked at the door and tried to plan an escape. Because of my longing to be in the back, I would have had to climb off the bike, try and maneuver my way through the rest of people and bikes, pass the instructor and leave.

You can do this. You'll get used to it.

My pep talks did no good. We began slowly with a warm up. The teacher instructed us to go at her pace and gave signals when the movement changed.

A few years ago, I rode a horse. Don't get me wrong, I have nothing against horses but the thought of riding one again brings me back to a dark place. To begin with, it's not like the movies. You don't simply jump on a horse. They are tall. Also, I have no capability

194

to jump. My boyfriend at the time was making an attempt to do something different by taking me horseback riding, which in itself was a major change for him but he had no idea how much I would hate it.

They had to bring in a step stool, so I could mount the horse. Again, I was pretty overweight, so I was humiliated because I felt like everyone was staring at me and what was worse, I was worried once I finally *did* get on the horse, it would promptly buck me off because I was too heavy. I essentially *rolled* onto the horse and once I was finally up there, hard leather seat between my legs, it was completely terrifying. I never felt stable. Not only that but it hurt. I was sore the next day.

I found myself in a similar situation years later at Treasure Island in Las Vegas when I suddenly decided to fulfill my curiosity and ride a mechanical bull. It wasn't crowded and since it was only my mother that was with me, I thought I'd give it a shot.

Once again, the experience was not what I expected. I'd seen people do this on TV and in movies and never once did the actor have a difficult time getting on the bull. Mechanical bulls are in the center of what is essentially a blow up fun house. The bouncy material doesn't provide much stability to give you the strength to jump on the bull.

Wearing jeans and a long sleeve purple shirt, I made my way into the center. I was bouncing a bit as I walked and almost immediately questioned my decision to ride the bull as I was approaching it. Thinking I could just hop on, I pressed both feet into the surface and attempted to jump on top. My stomach hit the midsection of the bull. I hadn't even gotten close. I decided my first attempt wasn't the best I could do.

I went for it again. This time, I was able to throw my hand to the top of the bull. I grabbed it and dug my claws in, trying to reach the rope so I could climb my way up and not hit the ground. I hung there for a moment before I let myself drop.

This little circus went on for a few minutes. Once the bull operator had enough entertainment, he raised the head of the bull up in the air, so his butt was low enough to climb on. I was going to have to come in from the back.

Once I was able to straddle the back, I had to shimmy my way to the front where the rope was. Even though I've seen plenty movies to know that only one hand goes up, my initial instinct was to hold on with both hands, but the operator quickly corrected me.

I'm certain the process of getting on the bull didn't take as long as I thought it did but, in that moment, I felt as if time had slowed down and I would never recover from the psychological damage that I had incurred.

The first few seconds were easy. The bull shifted softly to the right and left, then up and down. Just when I had decided that I was borderline enjoying myself, the operator revealed a more sinister side. He sped the bull up and suddenly it was bucking violently. I could feel my skin shifting and I knew my belly and thighs were jiggling away. Somewhere in the middle of that, he began to make the bull vibrate with a great level of intensity. I felt my double chin doing a dance for the entire restaurant.

The truth was, I could have held on a few seconds longer, but I was feeling embarrassed, a rare emotion for me. I plopped down onto the bouncy surface, rolled over and carefully got to my feet.

I shot the bull operator a deadly look. Luckily when I took a look around the ring, I noticed that my mother was the only audience I had. When I finally got over to her, she was just beginning the process of stifling her laughter. I asked to see the video she had taken (at my request) immediately. Nothing will make you feel less adequate about your weight than watching yourself ride a mechanical bull. The video was worse than I thought. If my mother were evil, she'd have quite the blackmail material but luckily only a very few people have seen that footage.

I bring those two stories up for a reason. I would gladly ride 10 horses and 15 mechanical bulls each day for the rest of my life if it meant I didn't have to feel the pain of the first spin class I took. The leather saddle of a horse and the hard exterior of a mechanical bull pale in comparison to the misery I felt on top of that bicycle seat.

It feels like the fist of a robot is repeatedly punching you in your private parts. I would welcome the moments in which we were instructed to stand up and pretend we were climbing up a hill in our bikes because it gave me some reprieve. I tried sitting in a number of positions. I pushed my vagina back to the back of the seat. I brought it forward. I sat with my butt sticking up high in the air but none of it worked.

I actually considered crying, but I managed to make it through without having a break down. As soon as class was over, I vowed never to return. If the class wasn't bad enough, the day after made it even worse as my walk had clearly indicated.

Each step was painful and every time I sat in a chair or on the toilet I let out a little yelp. This punishment lasted for over a week. I had literally bruised my vagina and I didn't even think that was something that could happen.

Fast forward 11 years. My bestie Cassandra and I joined a new gym and since she wasn't aware of the travesty I went through, she told me she wanted to try it.

At first, I scoffed at the idea. I told her what I had been through and that I still had post-traumatic stress disorder from the first time. She mentioned it consistently and I finally considered it since I was in better shape and that I was much lighter than I was in college.

I agreed to go again. I went when my favorite teacher was the instructor and did a bit of research. We walked in and the scene was all too familiar. It was dark and there were people just casually spinning. The instructor saw me, and I flat out told her I was concerned about the welfare of my vagina. This didn't seem to faze her. She told me that happened to everyone and that essentially, I had to do it a few times a week for my private areas to adjust. I told her I wasn't sure I could commit to a few times a week of pure torture.

She told us the importance of adjusting the seat correctly and helped us but even with her guidance, I felt the familiar pain when I got on the bike. My friend agreed that it was painful but that the calories burned made it worth it. We tried it one more time after that, but it never got better. I genuinely began to worry that it would ruin sex or reproduction for me. The seat rubbed so aggressively that I was confused by the sensation at times. In the end, I decided I hated it and I haven't been since. I always see it on the schedule of classes, but I skip right over it and decide I don't have the time to work it in to my life. Unless I find a padded adult diaper that I can wear, I don't anticipate spin ever being a part of my routine.

Softball

I wasn't an athletic kid. Actually, this is an understatement. If anything, I was the antithesis of athletic. People actually talked about how slow I was all the time. Other than riding my bike, I didn't really like being outside. There weren't a lot of kids in my neighborhood and by that, I mean there were zero kids in my neighborhood, so I spent most of my time inside teaching my stuffed animals how to spell.

I did have school friends though and those friends played softball. This intrigued me so one day I informed my parents that I wanted to play too. They were skeptical at first because as I said, I wasn't born with an athletic bone in my body. In fact, the only experience I had with softball was when I accidentally ran into a softball bat mid-swing when I was at my babysitter's house as a small child.

My father had come to pick up me up and because I was excited to see him, I started running. He watched as I sprinted toward him. The teenage girl practicing her swing didn't see me and right as I ran past her, she took a swing and landed the bat right on my forehead. I fell to the ground as a chunk of my head went flying. That little mistake prompted a bloody ride to the hospital, a terrified set of parents and 60 stitches. I still have the scar which I now pretend came from Voldemort (*Harry Potter* reference number two if you need to run and get a shot from your liquor cabinet).

In spite of my rough history with softball bats and my lack of ability, my parents signed me up to play in a local league in Chattanooga when I was 5 years old. I remember walking up to the first team I had been assigned to play on. The girls on the team were whipping the ball back and forth to each other quickly and looked like tiny professionals.

Prior to that day, I hadn't even put my hand in a glove. My parents bought me a glove, heated it, and tried to make it ready but it was still pretty stiff. I was introduced to the coach and then paired up with another member of the team and instructed to throw the ball back and forth until practice started.

I didn't know the rules of softball or what I was doing at all. I missed every ball that was thrown at me. I didn't miss it gracefully either. She was firing the balls at me and since I wasn't confident with the glove I dodged the ball by moving my arms and legs around and putting the glove in front of my face. The worst part was when I attempted to throw it back. The best versions of throws that I had were when I threw it and it fell about half way between the two of us. Those were good because they were in the center. For the most part, I threw wildly. It's like my arm wouldn't listen to my brain and the ball would end up 20 feet to the right or in some cases behind me.

Once the horrific practice was over, the coach basically told my parents I would be better suited for a less competitive league. Essentially, I was kicked off. It was fine by me because the whole experience was a bit traumatizing. I ended up playing for a more localized and beginner-friendly league a bit further away from where we lived. The best part was, I ended up playing with my childhood best friend.

In this league, I wasn't the only beginner and that made a big difference. With a bit of practice on the field and at home, I started to grasp the basics. For the first couple years, I served as backup for the right field position.

I wasn't quite the player that picked dandelions and chased butterflies, but I was close. Balls didn't come to me often but when they did, I missed them most of the time. I hit occasionally but I would always get out on first base. To be honest, I was bad. I liked playing though. I thought it was fun to be out there and I would patiently wait for my turn to play.

When I was around 8, my father decided to start his own team. He was my coach; our jerseys were purple, and we were called the Mustangs. My Dad favored me of course but he knew that I wasn't an all-star. It was during this time that he tried putting me in as catcher.

At that age, being catcher was great because there were very few high-pressure situations and I was involved in pretty much every play. He rotated between me and another girl, but I got playing time every game. Before long, I could throw from home plate to second and stopped most everything that came by me. I wouldn't go so far as to say that I was "good." I still only got sportsmanship awards rather than all-star spots or MVP trophies, but I did my job.

I loved playing softball and played for years. When we moved to Tuscaloosa, I joined a youth league in Cottondale where we lived. I played catcher for that team as well and I had a couple memorable moments. I tagged someone out in a standoff at home and actually got a hit off of the most talented pitcher in the league. Once I got into the teen years though, it was time to either quit or try out for the high school team.

My parents didn't have a lot of money and I wasn't sure I could make the team or whether or not I wanted to, so I decided to hang up my cleats for good. Looking back, I wonder how different life would have been had I kept playing. I wondered if I would have the same weight issues, but I guess it's pointless to reminisce in that way.

I thought my softball days were over until I became an adult and the church and work leagues became popular. I tried a couple church leagues, but I was never really allowed to play on those because other people were chosen first. I also had a bit of a foul language problem that made the church games a bit awkward. I may or may not have gotten scolded once or twice by a ref.

I was at my heaviest weight when I was approached about a softball team where I worked several years ago. I was apprehensive because I was so insecure about my weight and knew it had been years since I played. On the other hand, it was enticing to revisit a piece of my childhood and I also thought it may be a nice way to get some exercise in since I wasn't doing a whole lot of that at the time. I'm not usually a "joiner" but I decided to give it a shot.

I knew I was in trouble when the company shirts were distributed. The trim was blue, and a large flaming baseball leapt from the cotton with my number 84, on the front and the back.

"Attention! Attention, please!" screeched the over-achieving, team building, human resource director, "All of the games are going to be held at Bowers Park and they start in a couple of weeks, so I think that 5 or 6 practices before then should be enough and please make sure to wear navy shorts."

"Bowers Park? There will be 100 people there. And...shorts? We have to wear shorts? And practice?!" I said all of this in pure disbelief. I couldn't imagine my unsightly spider veins and to be frank, my very bright, white legs on display like a giant block of fresh mozzarella at the deli.

"Yes," said the HR Director, "and you are going to be switching between the positions of catcher and extra person."

I'm not saying it's always the case but it's no surprise that I was going to be playing catcher. Had the coach heard that I was a catcher extraordinaire in my childhood youth? No, I was chubby, and it isn't a secret that chubby girls were often stuck in the catcher position because it didn't require running. There was a lot of running in the outfield positions for adult teams because people often hit the slow-pitched ball far out into the field. There are a lot of home runs in adult, slow-pitch softball games.

Now, skipping the two weeks in which I "forgot" about practice and banked my salvation from humiliation on remaining the "extra" person, I will go right into the night of the first event. Had I known that exactly 10 of the 32 people that had signed up for the team would show up on the first game, I would have probably reconsidered.

From bottom to top, I looked rough: Old, worn tennis shoes that gained wear from a brief "running" phase, ankle socks (or in my case cankle socks), navy shorts, my company shirt, and a very high ponytail with several clips to keep my stringy bangs from my eyes.

"You're late and you're wearing glasses. You can't play softball in glasses, Heather." The coach was also the company CEO. I didn't even know he knew my name.

"I can't see without them. Besides, I am the EP," embracing an attempted abbreviation of my bench warming status.

"Well, practically no one showed up so, without you we will have to forfeit," he said as if he really needed me to pull this out for the company, "So, catcher it is. Let's go. The game is about to start."

Oh my God. Oh my God. This was my repeated phrase while I moseyed behind the plate with people screaming, "Hustle!" in the stands.

The CEO had already warmed up with someone else, so I got one warm up pitch. One. He pitched it to me and I caught it. Well, I threw my body in front of it, but I think that counts. I figured I could make that my strategy, flailing my body in front of the ball. Potentially letting it hit me time and time again seemed like an easier solution than chasing the ball around each pitch.

I had not, however, figured out how I was to get the ball from the plate to the pitcher's mound without seriously injuring myself, so I thought, *here goes,* and I heaved the ball as a shot put thrower heaves with all their might and watched it bounce about four or five feet in front of the CEO because of course the man in control of my job would be pitcher and I would have to interact with him every time.

Damn

"Ok darlin', throw as hard as you can sweetie," he said with a weird combination of disgust and pity on his face. I figured I would probably lose my job, especially when I shouted, "Scoot up if you want me to get it to you!" after I had heard enough "sweeties" and "honeys" for one night.

I decided squatting wasn't for me, so I sort of bent over a little with my glove held out as far as I could reach because I was standing a good 6 feet behind the plate. I never let one get by me. To this day I think I still have a mark from an unfortunate foul ball but at least I didn't have to look into the patronizing face of the umpire one single time.

I made it through the game somehow mostly unscathed. I winced every time the ball was hit, wiped flecks of red mud from my face and legs and was fairly certain I would have to do the same from my behind when I got home.

The final score of that first game was 24-4 and it was not in our favor. I came to a few more games over the next couple of seasons when the coach came by with a voice of desperation in his voice, telling me that I was the only hope preventing them from forfeiting. He would always say it in that tone, "This is going to hurt me far more than it's going to hurt you."

Within a couple seasons, the team went from co-ed to all male and they recruited players from other places who didn't work for the company. I haven't played softball since.

Swimming

When I was a child, I had a constant case of Swimmer's Ear. I am certain that I've had at least a mild ear infection for 30 straight years. I have never had a doctor who examined my ears not tell me that they are red. I assume it comes from the allergies I've always had but any time I swam as a child, I got terrible infections.

I refuse to swim in lakes because the one time I did, I swam in Lake Tuscaloosa with a church group and in the following days, I began to feel a horrible ear infection coming on. I called my doctor every day, trying to make an appointment and was told I would need to go to the emergency room. I finally yelled at them and said that there was no point in having a primary care physician if they wouldn't see me. I tried to explain that this wasn't your typical ear infection.

By the time I was allowed an appointment (to which they acted like I should scrub their feet clean with my tongue because they squeezed me in), I drove myself to the doctor. It takes a lot for me to go to the doctor because I'm pretty stubborn about forking out money for a co-pay. I had tears in my eyes, I couldn't hear, and my entire face was swollen. I had called into work, which I never did, but because I was a telephone operator and there was some type of substance leaking out of my ears, I thought it would be best. I even asked my mother to come sit with me.

Two hours later, I was able to see the doctor. When he stuck the tool into my ear, I almost threw up from pain. "My God, I've never seen an ear infection this bad. You should have come in long before this." The look I gave him prompted a terrified expression on his face. "I have been trying for days to get in." He later took responsibility for their lack in service and said he was going to try to get me an appointment with an ear, nose, and throat doctor within the next hour or they were going to have to admit me into the hospital.

I felt validated at that point. That shit was serious and to this day I think it's the sickest I've ever been. I realize I'm fortunate I've never had anything worse in life but I'm a huge baby when I'm sick, so you can only imagine how I was acting then.

Luckily, the doctor was able to make me an immediate appointment, so we went down the road to the ENT. He was also impressed by the magnitude of my ear infection. He inserted what he called an "ear tampon" into my ear canal because it had swollen completely shut and used this vacuum thing to suck out the wax and infection. It was as awful as it sounds.

He also gave me some pretty sweet pain medication that allowed me to sleep through the rest of the ear infection. Since then,

I've been highly cautious about the water that I get in. I have never stepped foot in another lake and when I'm in the ocean, I don't let the water get above my waist.

As an adult, I started searching for a type of exercise that didn't have quite the impact of running or high impact classes. My knees had been bothering me because I was still at the beginning of my weight loss journey and I needed something else.

My mother used to teach water aerobics at the YMCA when I was in my early college years. She absolutely loved it. It was a low impact, challenging workout that burned a ton of calories. She pressured me to try it and so I did. When I went, I was the youngest person in the class by about 60 years (excluding my mom) and while I enjoyed it in some ways, I simply could not keep going. I wasn't popular by any means and I'm not one to be too embarrassed to do things with my mother but going to a water aerobics class with my mom and 6 other older women while a skinny cute lifeguard my age watched was even more than I could handle.

When I started being serious about fitness though, I reconsidered. I went to the local PARA and joined. I was looking for a gym and at $100 for the entire year, PARA was the best solution. They had a weight room with several types of fitness equipment, but they also had a pool. I didn't really want to do water aerobics, but I noticed that they had an open lap schedule early in the morning. I thought that would be something great to try before work.

So, I dusted off my one-piece bathing suit and headed to PARA one morning at 6AM. I put on my suit and as usual, hated myself in it. I was, of course, overweight and hadn't worn the suit in a long time so it was too small. The undercarriage of my stomach peeked out through the leg holes and the whole thing was just a mess. I decided that I would proceed anyway and try to get a new bathing suit later.

I dropped my belongings off in a locker and walked out to the pool. I noticed a couple of the lanes were already taken but the one closest to me was not. I walked carefully toward the pool with my hands over my belly.

"Ma'am!" yelled a lifeguard that couldn't have been over 16 years old.

I looked up at him and a wave of fear came over me.

"Ma'am. You *need* to shower before you get in the pool. You can't just walk in there. You have to wash off."

That was one of the fattest moments I can recall in my recent memory. I mean I realize that everyone has to wash off before they get in the pool (though I didn't know that then) but the way he said it, as if I needed to wash the nasty off of me before I could get in the highly chlorinated pool made me feel exposed and disgusting.

"Uh, ok." I noticed the shower for the first time after that and walked over to it, turning the water on. The lifeguard kept his eye on me, which was also awkward. I wondered if he was thinking about how fat I was. I also wasn't sure how long I needed to shower. Should I say my ABCs like they say to do when brushing my teeth or was a different amount of time appropriate?

I bathed off until he lost focus and made my way over, stepping gingerly down the stairs into the pool. I started swimming immediately. I don't think I had really ever swum laps before. I had raced in the pool plenty of times as a kid but there weren't many opportunities to have a lane to myself and just swim. I'm a good swimmer in that my freestyle form is correct. My parents got me swim lessons when I was young, so I know how to swim well. I am, however, extremely slow. It kind of looks like I'm doing the freestyle swimming motion and an invisible person is standing there beside me, holding my waist so I can't go anywhere.

I began swimming and made it to the end of the Olympic sized pool. I didn't know how to flip so I just turned around and headed for the other side. About halfway through that lap, I started to feel fatigued. I hadn't even been there five minutes but in that amount of time, every muscle I had was exhausted. I was both pleased and worried about this because I knew it would be a great workout, but I wasn't sure if I had the stamina to stick around more than 10 minutes a day.

Each day I went, I started to swim longer and longer. There were two older women who also came every morning. I told my friend that I got to see all kinds of "grandginas" in the morning so if you ever hear anyone say that, know that I invented that term. Over time, they started talking to me and flexing their maternal muscles.

"You need goggles." One of the women said one day.

"Oh, I'm OK. I can see underwater." I said awkwardly back to her as we were both basically naked in the locker room.

"Doesn't matter. You will hurt your eyes."

"Ok. I'll get some this weekend."

The next day, she brought me a spare pair of goggles and said that I could keep them. I will admit that it helped but sometimes when I went to take them off, it felt like they were going to suck the eyeballs out of my head.

A couple weeks after that she said, "You need a swim cap. You are going to destroy your hair."

Well, that wasn't going to happen. I mean, goggles I can get on board with but stuffing all my hair and my fat head into essentially a condom was out of the question.

The old woman begged to differ though and the next day, she brought me a swim cap.

"It's pink."

"Yes, I see that. Thank you."

I already had a mother. I didn't need this woman taking control of my life. But like my mother, she was annoyingly right yet again. The swim cap made the entire process more pleasant. The chlorine *was* doing a number on my hair.

After a couple months, I discovered that I really loved going. It was a great way to wake me up in the mornings before work. It was a full body workout and it didn't hurt my joints. Unfortunately, once I decided I would continue doing it, my ears started to ache. The pain begun as more of a nagging annoyance than anything but then the feeling was all too familiar. I skipped a couple days then when I went back, I brought earplugs with the hope that they would be the solution I needed.

Unfortunately, the ear pain only grew worse and I knew that I would more than likely have to give up my dreams of being the next Summer Sanders. It was fun while it lasted but as I've gotten older I now know that swimming for me has to be limited to the few times I manage to get in a bathing suit in the summer time. It's not often but it does happen occasionally.

What's the point?

The point in telling you about the exercises and embarrassment I've been through, lead me to find the exercises I could do on a consistent basis. Listen, I sweat profusely, have a difficult time sitting in plane seats, get nervous to get on theme park rides (because I have been kicked off one for being overweight) and contemplate not doing anything that requires a scale. Life is one, giant, embarrassing shit show.

This world is not made for people who are not thin. It's just a fact. Who CARES what other people think? I've found that for me, I like to hike (when it's not hot) and hit things (translation: kickboxing). Find what you can do.

Find what doesn't hurt in a bad way. Find something that doesn't bore you to death. Take care of your body the best way you know how because you know what? You are the only one that can determine that.

Be honest with who you are and wake up every day making a choice to love yourself, make better decisions and stop waiting on yourself to be perfect.

Make Salads Fun Again

Chicken Salad

The word salad can be quite a trickster. Take a gander at the fat and calories in the chicken salad at your favorite spot. The numbers are more than likely so absurd you feel like they can't be right. The primary culprit: mayonnaise. Y'all. I love mayo. I love it slathered on a sandwich or mixed into some of my favorite southern concoctions. But, it's just not "good" for us. I'm so sorry. Sometimes, you may have to splurge on the real stuff but there are ways to make tasty chicken salad at home. Fat free mayonnaise is an abomination in the eyes of the Lord. Low fat isn't ideal but it's acceptable. Use low fat. This recipe will make several sandwiches throughout the week unless you're me and eat it all in one sitting.

Ingredients:

- 1 rotisserie chicken (These are readily available at almost every grocery store. Don't make your own. These have great, built in flavor)
- 1 half chopped medium sized Vidalia onion (chopped small if you don't want big pieces of onion)
- 1 green onion, sliced
- 1 tablespoon minced garlic
- 1 mandarin orange, sliced
- 10 seedless purple grapes, halved

212

- 2 tablespoons chopped almonds
- 2 tablespoons low fat mayonnaise
- 2 tablespoons non-fat Greek yogurt
- Salt, pepper, garlic powder to taste

Directions:

When the rotisserie chicken is cool enough to handle, remove the skin, take the meat off the bones, and break up all the chicken with your hands.

You can buy the chicken ahead of time but go ahead and take the meat off when it's warm. It's much easier. You can save it in the fridge until you're ready.

Once you've gotten the chicken pulled off and in a large bowl, just throw literally every ingredient in the bowl and mix together.

This goes well on bread, in a wrap, on top of lettuce or just by itself.

Leftover Pork Chop Cornbread Salad

I didn't make that sound appealing, did I? Sure, you don't have to use leftovers but that is how this salad came about. If you'd like, you can grill the pork chops and prepare fresh cornbread, but I recommend having pork chops and cornbread one night and then using the leftovers the next day to make this salad. It's yum. Maybe you made the Honey Soy Pork Chops served with cornbread from earlier one night? Use any leftovers from that to make this salad the next day.

Ingredients:

- 2-3 ounces leftover pork chops
- Lettuce (however much you'd like)
- 1 Large Piece Leftover Cornbread
- 1 Chopped onion (to taste)
- ½ sliced cucumber
- ¼ cup shredded low fat Cheddar Cheese
- 1 tablespoon low fat butter spread
- 2 to 3 tablespoons Homemade Skinny Ranch (recipe at the beginning of book)

Directions:

In a large, non-stick skillet heat 1 tablespoon of butter spread to a pan on medium heat on one side. While it heats up, cut both cornbread and pork chops into cubes. Add cornbread to the side with the butter and pork chop bites to the other side to heat through. Flip the cornbread over and move it around for a few minutes until crispy. While that is happening, chop up your onion, slice your cucumber and prepare your lettuce. Assemble your vegetables and then add the pork chop bites and the cornbread "croutons" to the top. Serve it with the skinny dressing or whatever dressing you'd like. It puts a wonderful spin on your leftovers.

Asian Chicken Salad

The key to making chicken less boring is adding lots of flavor. It's important to know that flavor doesn't necessarily mean fat. Adding a spicy flare to your food makes your mind think that you are getting something more decadent. That's why I love spicing things up with Asian or Mexican flavors.

Ingredients:

- 1 grilled chicken breast
- 1 teaspoon chili sauce
- 1 tablespoon peanut sauce
- 2 tablespoons ginger sesame dressing
- 2 tablespoons reduced fat Feta Cheese
- 3-4 Kalamata olives (chopped and also optional. I put olives in everything. I've also added grilled corn to this salad which was another great addition)
- Sliced red onion (amount up to you)
- 2 tablespoons chopped peanuts
- 1 tablespoon toasted sesame seeds
- 1 chopped green onion

Directions:

If you haven't already, grill or bake the chicken breast. Once the chicken is grilled, you are ready to assemble the salad. Toss the chicken in the chili sauce and peanut sauce. Lay it on top of a bed of lettuce. Add the peanuts, dressing, feta, olives, sesame seeds, red onion slices and green onions.

Crunchy Shrimp Salad

Ingredients:

- Fresh shrimp, tails on, that have been peeled and deveined (if you are making it for yourself, don't skimp on the shrimp. It's not bad for you)
- Lettuce
- 1 tablespoon olive oil
- 1 pinch salt
- 1 pinch pepper
- 1 pinch smoked Paprika
- 2 tablespoons reduced fat Blue Cheese
- 2 tablespoons light Balsamic Vinaigrette
- 5 pita chips that you've crushed

Directions:

Marinate shrimp in olive oil, salt, pepper, and paprika. You can prepare your shrimp by putting them on kabobs and grilling them or by sautéing them in a non-stick skillet. I like the flavor that the grill provides but either way is fine.

While the shrimp cooks, prepare a plate with your favorite lettuce, add the blue cheese and crushed pita chips, and then add the cooked shrimp.

Drizzle the dressing over the top and that's all there is to this salad. I make this salad big since it's healthy.

Steak and Blue Cheese Salad

Ingredients:

- 3-five ounce Flat Iron steak or lean Sirloin
- ½ lettuce
- 1 tablespoon olive oil
- 1 pinch salt
- 1 pinch pepper
- 1 pinch garlic powder
- 2 tablespoons reduced fat Blue Cheese
- 2 tablespoons homemade low-cal Ranch (located earlier in the book)
- 1 to 2 tablespoons canned onion straws

Directions:

Marinate steak in olive oil, salt, pepper, and garlic. You can prepare your steak by sautéing it in a non-stick skillet or grilling it for about 3 minutes on either side.

Let the steak rest while you prepare the rest of the ingredients. Prepare a plate with your lettuce of choice, add the ranch dressing and blue cheese.

Slice the steak into thin strips and add it to the salad.

Top it with the onions for crunch. This version is way healthier than what you may find at a steak house.

12

Resources That Motivate

It's hard out there in this lonely world. Hating your body is a supremely isolating feeling. It doesn't matter if those close to you also share harmful body image and masochistic ways. Their story is different from yours. When I read *Hunger*, by Roxane Gay, I wanted it to be a book that encouraged body acceptance. I wanted it to reach me in ways that would help me on my path to being comfortable in my own skin. At the very least, I thought that it would be relatable in a sense that I hadn't felt before.

As I was reading it, I grew more and more frustrated by the book. First of all, she was talking about something I'd never seen before in non-fiction. It's something that I wanted to talk about in my book, so I was offended that she was discussing being overweight in a fashion that wasn't about the traditional ideas of success v. failure. That was *my* shtick. As I kept reading, I didn't feel hopeful at all. I resonated with a lot of the discomfort she talked about, living in a world that doesn't accommodate fat people, but felt alienated because she labeled someone of my size as "Lane Bryant" fat. I was so confused after reading the book. It wasn't helpful at all.

It wasn't until I realized that I was reading Gay's book under the guise of a self-help book. What's obnoxious about that is I know better than to do that. I still function under the mentality of "fixing" myself. What book can I read, what diet can I follow, who can I worship in order to love my body (while also being skinny). The way I compute how I feel about my body and the way I treat it is a mental hurtle that cannot be solved by reading one book.

Roxane Gay told *her* story. It wasn't mine to take and conform it into my own story. Roxane Gay isn't an inspiration because she's conquered this whole self-love thing, she's an inspiration because she's been through hell and was brave enough to use her voice and talent to tell the world about it. It doesn't matter that it wasn't the key to my future success.

The word inspiration is a towering, intimidating word that we, as a society, put too much stock in. After starting my blog, people began to discuss it with me. Anytime someone has approached me in a public setting about the blog I become a shell of my former self. I start to look at the floor, stutter and awkwardness fills every nook and cranny of the room like a painful, uncomfortable gas.

I can't stand discussing anything I write with people. I realize avoiding these conversations is impossible when I post everything I write to the Internet but I legit start itching all over and immediately try to change the subject. Mostly, my discomfort stems from being incapable of taking a compliment. Most of the time, people are being very kind about what I write. I don't feel worthy of their accolades.

Once I began losing a significant amount of weight, the constant barrage of pleasantries made me want to crawl inside the blubber of the weight I'd lost and never leave. The most horrifying word that people used: inspiration.

The woman in particular that I used to work with that began her own weight loss journey and attributed her motivation to me is a prime example. Just as she was lighting a fire, I was losing speed. I hated when I ran into her at work. It wasn't *her*. It was the fact that I knew she would start gushing about my accomplishments and tell me that I was the reason she began to get healthy. I knew I'd lost a lot of weight, but I never felt satisfied. I hadn't reached my goal and it was getting harder and harder to lose or even maintain. I had already begun wallowing in my failure mentality. How could someone who couldn't reach her goal, a failure, be anyone's inspiration?

Ultimately, inspiration to get healthy can only come from within. There's such a fine line between treating your body with respect while also not beating yourself up. I may have been an inspiration to some people and I'll probably never be comfortable with that but anyone who saw my story and got motivated, still reached within themselves to find that drive.

I don't think it's smart to put all of your eggs in one person's basket to motivate you. It's kind of like when you start a workout regimen with a friend. Over the years I've been workout partners with Cassandra for a number of different workout fads. It's been awesome but because of our schedules, we often don't get to go together. It's easy to stop going to the gym just because your friend can't go when you do. Then one thing leads to another and it's been a year since you've worked out.

221

Relying on someone or a book or a movie or a TV show to "save" you from your body is a bad idea. Having said that, finding encouraging resources is never a bad idea.

For example, I've already mentioned Geneen Roth and her book *Breaking Free from Emotional Eating.* It was liberating reading a book that was not recommending a specific diet. I found so much of what she was saying refreshing. Having said that, it wasn't a perfect solution. Some of the book was dated and the idea of giving up dieting and just eat when you're hungry was a bit too good to be true. Not only that, she touted her conferences as an additional way to "breaking free."

Well, I checked into them, and let's just say "breaking free" sure as shit isn't without cost. There is always a grace period after I read a self-help book where I become a worshipper of that text. I tried eating only when I was hungry after reading this book. It worked. I ate slow. I never ate standing up. I put my fork down after every bite. And the second I felt satisfied, I quit eating. This worked for less than a week before the "eat what you want, when you want" mantra overshadowed the part where she said to stop when you're full. Nothing was off the table and I was gaining weight. Then I found myself mad at Roth and myself for failing yet again. I should have read the book, not depended on it to fix my mind and body.

Roth is a good resource. So, is Jen Sincero, who wrote *You are a Badass.* The book's subtitle is "How to stop doubting your greatness and start living an awesome life." I was *so* into this. Sincero is funny and straightforward and makes a ton of great points. I was ready to kick ass and take over the world after reading certain pages. I think everyone that reads that book is accommodating a specific area in their life they'd like to change. The book is supposed to be all encompassing, but I read it because I didn't have a financial plan and I was drowning in debt with no end in sight.

Some of her suggestions flat out didn't seem feasible. She talked about hiring a life coach or paying someone to take away certain tasks that were bogging you down from reaching your goals. Well, the idea that I would have enough money to pay someone to get me through life was not only unlikely, it was ludicrous. I could barely afford to put gas in my car after I paid the minimum balance on my credit cards. There was no "extra" income.

My disappointment that the book in its entirety wasn't solving my problems was insurmountable. I thought she was cool. I thought she *got* me. I should have just taken a couple key thoughts from the book that helped me the most and ran with the rather than feeling the book was a miss for me.

When it comes to eating healthy food, my go-to is Lisa Lillien, otherwise known as "The Hungry Girl." I am such a fangirl for her. She is the master of quick tricks to make food healthier. Not only does she come up with genius ways to satisfy my cravings for "bad" foods, she understands the need for a realistic portion. This is my favorite part about her recipes. She knows how hangry the masses are and she creates recipes that make me feel full which is the key for me when I'm dieting.

There's nothing worse in the diet world than feeling hungry. Lillien has a ton of critics because she doesn't always use "clean" ingredients. While she has reformed her shtick to better meet the needs of the masses that require more natural ingredients, Lillien made a name for herself creating fast, convenient recipes that oftentimes include processed foods.

I understand *why* it's important to limit processed foods; I also know that the majority of the nation doesn't have the time or resources to always eat organic food. I'm totally on board with using a tub of whipped cream, fiber cereal, store bought, sugary ice cream cones, and whatever else to make a fast, filling dinner. In fact, many of the recipes I've concocted over the years had her in mind.

The only place Lillien and I don't see eye to eye is that I have never believed that "diet" food compares to the real thing. I think it's swell if you've come up with a low fat ranch dressing. To imply that a low fat version of ranch can remotely be on the same plane as the magnificent, creamy, perfect concoction where my blog got its namesake, is actually an insult to who I am as a person.

Listen clearly. Full fat ranch is on a level all by itself. It's not the only thing there will never truly be a substitute for...alternative versions of pizza, fried chicken, ice cream, etc. are fine but they aren't as good. They never will be. At least not for me. Sometimes, the fact is, the only thing that will satisfy your craving for a huge vat of buffalo wings and ranch dressing is a huge fucking vat of buffalo wings and ranch dressing.

It's OK to saddle up as many resources as you need to learn about the direction you want to head as long as you know that just because someone says they have the answer doesn't mean they have all the answers for *you*. I sure as shit don't have all the answers. It has taken me a long time to realize that life is hard, and you have to find a multitude of resources to cope with it. This past year was the first time I started seeing a therapist. I wanted her to fix me. I was anxious constantly and for the first time my anxiety was turning into depression. I have gained nearly half the weight I lost. Every week I try to find new motivation. I find myself desperate to lose weight. I feel like a failure. That failure affects my relationships. I worry that Ian will leave me or that I don't deserve his love because I'm fat and disgusting. When I was writing my book, I felt inauthentic. How could I possibly write about my weight loss journey when I didn't know what the hell I was doing anymore?

My therapist was about as green as they come. She was in graduate school, and she was the only therapy I could afford. She kept trying to get me to do exercises by the book. Some of the methods were helpful, some were not. Either way, she encouraged me to be more cognizant about the obsessive, negative thoughts I was having. She wanted me to take those thoughts, recognize them and then argue with them. I learned a great deal from that. I started recognizing how hard I was being on myself. I started realizing I didn't deserve that mistreatment.

Treatment isn't perfect. Pills aren't perfect. Books, articles, videos, etc. aren't perfect. While I think finding people who inspire/motivate are great, I still feel you should love yourself enough to know that every good thing that happens to your mind and body comes from within.

The most important thing you can do is not fall in the trap of some fad diet or self-help book. Read those books (especially Roxane Gay's) and soak them in but don't let them saturate you. They are told in someone else's voice, not yours. Love yourself, take advantage of those people in your support system and use the resources as sidekicks, not the main show. And once again, realize there's nothing wrong with you. Whatever your weight, job, financial situation, you don't need to be "fixed." We just all need a little help finding the best of who we are...one way or another.

I'll Take a Side of That!

Baked Fries

It is possible to make crispy fries in the oven but to my knowledge, it is not possible to do this without at least a small amount of oil.

Ingredients:

- 1 large Idaho potato (Yukon gold would work well too)
- 1 tablespoon olive oil
- 1 teaspoon garlic powder
- 1 teaspoon onion powder
- Salt, pepper, and grated Parmesan to taste

Note: All of these ingredients depend on how many people you have. I've done it for one person, and I've done it for two. If you have more, you can easily double, triple, or even quadruple the recipe.

Directions:

Preheat your oven to 375 degrees. While the oven is heating up, spray a non-stick cookie sheet (that you've covered in aluminum foil first).

THINLY slice the potato into French fry shapes. Try to be consistent in size and don't cut them too thick or they won't get crispy.

Once you have them all cut up, mix all ingredients in a bowl, and toss the potatoes until the oil and spices are evenly coated.

Then, spread them in a single layer on the cookie sheet. Pop them in the oven at least 30 minutes and then watch them to make sure they are crispy the way you like it.

Sometimes, if they are being stubborn, I'll turn the broiler on the last few minutes but if you do that be careful, they will burn in the blink of an eye.

Pro Tip: I like potato skins, so I rarely peel my potatoes. It gives a bit of extra fiber, too!

Zucchini/Potato Swirl

When I experimented with this recipe, I used what I had in my house. I had been seeing recipes for ratatouille everywhere and I thought they were so pretty. I didn't have tomatoes, eggplant or yellow squash and I don't eat peppers, so I went with what was in my fridge and that was zucchini, onions, and potatoes. You are welcome to use any of the above ingredients for more color/different flavors.

Ingredients:

- 1 yellow onion, chopped
- 3 zucchinis
- 4 potatoes (red or purple would be nice. I used plain ole baking potatoes. Just make sure you have about the same amount of potatoes and zucchini)
- 1 tablespoon of minced garlic
- Salt
- Pepper
- Garlic powder
- 2 tablespoons olive oil (divided)

Directions:

Pre-heat the oven to 375 degrees. While you wait, heat the tablespoon of olive oil in a skillet.

Add the chopped onions and sauté them until they are soft. While all that is going on, thinly slice the zucchini and potatoes into flat circles.

You can use a mandoline but beware that those are REALLY thin slices and will take you forever to alternate in your dish. I've done it both ways and I prefer doing the best I can to slice them thinly and about the same size.

Grab a round dish (pie pan will work) and spread the cooked onions on the bottom of the pan. Toss the potato and zucchini slices together in a bowl with oil and spices.

Then, beginning on the outside of the round dish, place the zucchini and olives upright and do it around the edge, alternating pieces and making a circle.

When the outer circle is done, continue inside of it, making another circle. Keep going until you reach the middle. Then, pop it in the oven.

If you have no potatoes, it doesn't take more than 30 minutes but if you do, depending on how thick your potato slices are, it could take 45 minutes to an hour and ten minutes.

When it comes out of the oven, you can sprinkle with cheese or green onions to add more flavor.

Pro Tip: Potatoes are annoyingly slow in the oven, but they are a staple. To save time you can microwave them a couple minutes before slicing.

Instant Mashed Potato Cakes

This recipe is perfect for people who are cooking for one or two. You are more than welcome to use fresh potatoes and mash them, but I find these instant cups of mashed potatoes in the grocery store. They have two servings, flavor, and all you do is add water and pop them in the microwave.

Ingredients:

- 1 cup instant mashed potatoes
- 1 teaspoon salt
- 1 teaspoon pepper
- 1 teaspoon garlic powder
- 1 tablespoon light butter spread
- 2 to 3 tablespoons chopped yellow onion
- 2 to 3 tablespoons shredded cheese (I use skim mozzarella or light sharp cheddar)
- 1 green onion, chopped
- Non-stick spray

Directions:

Heat butter in the skillet while the mashed potatoes are cooking in the microwave.

Take the mashed potatoes out of the microwave and put them in a bowl.

Combine other ingredients (except green onion) in bowl. Spray hands with the non-stick spray. Grab a small handful of the mixture and shape into a patty.

Make several of these and put them into a skillet and let them brown on both sides. When they are done, add a bit more salt and serve with green onions on top.

*The cool thing about these is that you can add anything to them (including meat) and/or top with a bit of light sour cream. They make a perfect side dish.

*If you want, another great idea is to skip the skillet and potato cakes and use the potato mixture as a dumpling filling. I've put it inside a wonton wrapper and baked them. Those are also tasty. You could eat them alone or put them in a soup.

13

Success vs. Failure

Well, we've moved to the climax of this little diatribe. I haven't reached the place of body image bliss and I don't have all the answers. I'm sorry to inform you of that. What I have done is taken inventory all of the tools I've used over the years and I've acknowledged what has worked and not worked and come to this conclusion: our view of success and failure in this society when it comes to body image is horrifyingly fucked up.

The fact that so many of us base our self-worth on how we look and what we weigh means that we set ourselves up for a constant cycle of failure. This mentality ravages both our physical and mental health.

These fears and doubts about our bodies manifest themselves in a number of ways. For me, one of the most obvious ways I express my disgust and "failure" with my body is through both emotional and binge eating.

Emotional and binge eating aren't mutually exclusive, but they are a little different. Emotional eating, according to WebMD, "means turning to food for comfort, not because you're hungry."

This is something I do. I eat as a response to almost every mood that I have. When I'm happy, I might say, "This has been a great day! I'm going to eat some cake." If I'm sad, I might say, "What a shitty day this has been! I'm going to eat some cake." In the few times I've slipped into depression that has lasted more than a few hours, I've been known to stock up on items like ice cream and cookie dough.

Even though I'm an emotional eater, I think I'm also a "make excuses eater." This isn't a technical term, but it is something that I do. Not only do I eat for comfort when I'm happy or sad, I also eat for comfort when my friends and family are happy or sad. I am pleased as punch if a friend desperately needs a margarita night because she is going through a breakup. What kind of friend would I be if I didn't help a pal in her time of need? I make excuses to eat and drink on birthdays, weddings, funerals, baby showers and pretty much any event that is a slight aversion to my daily routine. I am also bad about eating when I'm bored.

Before I was a full time teacher, I had several jobs, including an 8-5 Monday-Friday job, which meant that I never saw the benefits of summer or spring break until 2015 when I got the teaching gig as my sole job and had my first worthless summer. Sure, I had a side tutoring gig, I worked out, I wrote some and prepped for the fall semester but for the most part, I was inactive from the beginning of May until August. I certainly don't intend to complain.

How obnoxious would it be if I cried to you about not having to work in the summer when so many are still chugging away all week long? I won't do that. I will say though that I function best under stress and when I have a lot to do, so even though I slot out times during the summer to be somewhat productive on a daily basis, I am usually useless the rest of the time.

A couple summers ago, I re-watched every episode of both *Dawson's Creek* and *Sex and the City*. I hope you're not judging me as I'm sure all of you have guilty pleasures as well. When I'm lying in bed all day during the summer, I try and picture what types of food are in my cabinet every 20 minutes or so. I also stretch my domestic muscles as well because I'll just be lying there and suddenly feel like I need to cook.

Basically, summertime isn't good for me because if I'm doing well on my diet, the days last so long and it feels like I'm starving. If I slip on my diet, it's like letting a bull loose in a China shop. I'm running all around the kitchen looking for food to eat. I've had to make myself leave the house and go to coffee shops. Those can also be dangerous as I'm a sucker for a pastry.

In other words, it doesn't take much for me to find excuses to eat. I can do that any day, any hour, any minute. I definitely react to certain emotions with eating, but it's not limited to that. The biggest problem I have is when those moments that I eat for no reason occur, I often find myself binge eating. According to the Mayo Clinic, binge eating is "a serious eating disorder in which you frequently consume unusually large amounts of food and feel unable to stop eating." I've always been the type of person who goes beyond the feeling of satisfaction when I'm eating.

Being full doesn't stop me from continuing to stuff my face with food. I have eaten entire bags of potato chips, whole packs of cookies, pints of ice cream, etc. When I was a teenager, I would come home from school and ravage the cabinets when I got there. I remember biking to a friend's house in my neighborhood after school one day and she had shared her small snack with me. She told me that she was always hungry after school. Excited that I wasn't the only one, I started describing some of the food I usually ate when I got home. When I told her that I usually had chips, then Lucky Charms, she stopped me before I got to anything else and said with shock, "You have *two* snacks?!" I brushed it off and told her I was exaggerating but it was then I knew that I ate more than the average bear. Eating too much after school is probably normal at that age. When you're young and still growing, your body is always looking for more.

My problem with binge eating got excessive when I started dieting. I know that doesn't make sense but before I was dieting, eating "bad" food wasn't special to me. I ate what I wanted when I wanted. That was of course a problem that caused me to gain weight but when I started dieting, I coveted the treats that I wasn't usually allowed to have, making them more desirable and sacred. When I first started Weight Watchers, I made Sunday my "cheat day." This isn't a Weight Watchers thing, but I didn't count activity or flex points at first, so I just thought I was *owed* a cheat day. For the first 50 pounds or so, the cheat day didn't really affect my weight loss. I would bounce back immediately on Monday.

The problem was that no matter what variation of "cheat days," or cheat meals that I've designated for myself over the years, binge eating has always occurred. The Slow Carb diet allows one cheat day per week and when I first started I wanted to be like, "You just *think* you want people to have a cheat day. You don't even know what I am capable of eating in 12 hours."

When I have cheat days, I will make sure to get up early in the morning, so I can go ahead and start eating. I will have at least

3-4 huge meals and multiple snacks in between. A typical day may include a bacon, egg and cheese biscuit and large hash brown from any fast food place, about a dozen Oreos and some chips for a snack, about $15 worth of a place called Taco Casa in Alabama where I may have a Mexican Pizza, rice, nachos, etc., then I would have another snack, maybe some cheese or popcorn, then dinner at my parents in which I would have two, three or four helpings of food and then end it with dessert.

By the end of the night, I'm always so sick; I come close to literally vomiting. This was happening every Sunday. I have tried changing it over the years, so I allow myself two cheat meals a week or I find ways to split it up. I refuse to permanently give up things that I love but I also don't know how to pace myself. I have learned that I can't be trusted to eat what I want when I want it, but I haven't quite mastered a healthy balance. I have a personality that craves excess.

When I'm not limiting myself, in my mind I feel like I need to fit everything in that I can because I may not get it for a while. I do this for eating and drinking. Not only is this habit not healthy physically or emotionally, it's dangerous. At the end of a binge, my body has tried to purge in any way it can via reflux or vomit out of my mouth or it comes out the other direction (many times both). My chest will hurt, I'll have trouble walking and my whole body will ache. The silly part about all of it is that I know how it will affect me and yet I do it anyway all the time.

Weight isn't just about aesthetics. I would venture to say that the way I look is only a catalyst to a larger problem. The issues start in your mind and until you work on who you are as a person, it's unlikely you will ever make and maintain changes in your body. There are a multitude of resources and ideas out there to help you cope with bingeing and emotional eating. One of my problems is that if I'm not dealing with or rewarding myself with food, I'm doing it with spending money and that's not ideal either. I'm a writer and a teacher with mounds of debt so utilizing my free time by shopping is something I shouldn't do (though I seem to do it a lot).

Here are some activities to do rather than eat or spend money: exercise (even a quick walk will steer your brain from eating), pop in a piece of gum, do some kind of calming activity like meditation, take a hot bath, scream into a pillow, or punch someone in the face (just kidding). You can go into a Wikipedia worm hole and search something random. Stop procrastinating on a project around the house you've been wanting to do for a year. Plan your wedding or consider what you would do with a million dollars. Make positive affirmations, give your pet a bath, clean the house, read a book, stalk an old crush on social media or do anything else that can occupy your time.

Waiting on a food or money spending craving to pass is kind of like trying not to smoke. The cravings can be fierce and aggressive, but they don't stay. Sometimes you will have success with this and sometimes you won't. Neither makes you "good" or "bad."

Binge eating is a physical reaction to this flawed mentality of success versus failure. There are also severe mental ramifications. One of those for me happens to be intense fear. I live in fear of being too fat. I live in fear that my boyfriend will leave me. I live in fear that I will lose a limb from high blood sugar or that I will die of a heart attack.

I have other fears as well. Besides cockroaches and tornadoes, I have one major fear that sends shivers down my spine.

My fear of this object has been with me since my junior high years. Just seeing it makes me want to flee.

This fear is of the scale.

I know I'm not alone because there is actually a technical name for it: gravitophobia. According to *Psychology Today*, gravitophobia is the irrational fear of your bathroom scale. I have had many ups and downs with this disease. I used to be guilty of a daily weigh in. I also went years where I didn't weigh at all. Both of these angles are not healthy for you. The article on gravitophobia says it best, "Let me be clear. The scale isn't your friend or your enemy. The scale is just something to provide you with another piece of information with which to help you inform your decisions."

Sure, it's easy for a website to be all, "You shouldn't be scared of the scale" but yet, there I am on weigh-ins, naked and afraid just like the day I was born. Every time I go to the doctor I tell them I normally weigh naked and the shoes and jeans can't help and oh also, I had a big breakfast. They've heard every weight joke in the book, so they rarely acknowledge my quips. At home, I don't have a stitch of clothing on, I've tried my best to poop before I get on and I have been known to force myself to pee multiple times until the number I see resembles a number closer to what I want. I have gotten better over the years about my obsession with numbers, but I still skip the scale when I know it's "bad" and leap for it when I know there's a chance it's "good."

This is all a way for society to tell you what number you should be. After I had lost 70-80 pounds, I went to my doctor for a checkup. I've been seeing him every 6 months for at least a decade and he knows me well but every single time, he asks me if I exercise enough. It enrages me. All I want is for you to acknowledge that I've lost 70 pounds but no, you're all, "I mean are you just walking or are you working out?" He knows I exercise. Asshole.

Anyway, he once asked me if I had a goal weight. "Well, I mean, I'm sort of doing small goals right now so I won't get discouraged. I hadn't really thought about an ideal weight because I'm trying to get all of this figured out. You know what I mean, one day at a time. Is there a number you'd like to throw out there?" "Well, insurance says you should be 125." I stared at him for a second and then I just started laughing. "Well, insurance can get over it. That ain't happening." Frankly, I don't want to weigh 125 pounds. I think I would look sick at that weight. There are people who would want to lose more weight if they weighed 125 pounds, but those people are not *me*. If you ripped my right leg off right now, I guarantee you it would be at least 60-70 pounds. So, unless I become an amputee (god forbid), 125 is never a number I'm going to see on a scale again. I'm pretty sure I haven't seen it since 5th grade.

Obviously, fear of the scale is a fear that is a direct response from insecurity about weight. If all of that sounded familiar, it means you are relying too much on a number to relegate success or your happiness and you need to stop. I know it's easier said than done but there are other ways to tell if you are making progress. First, how do you feel? You know that eating healthy and exercise makes you feel better and that eating an entire pizza makes you feel crappy.

So, take note of how your body reacts physically to the food choices you are making. Also, your clothes will tell you if you are losing inches and really, the goal is to get new clothes anyway because yours are too baggy. You may be gaining muscle, so the scale shows a higher number but if you're jeans slide right over those hips when the week before you jumped around for five minutes trying to get in them, you're probably doing something right. Finally, try weighing once a month. If you can't hang with that, don't weigh more than once a week. Your body fluctuates tremendously based on a number of things including water retention. Don't get caught up in the numbers...also known as things I should tell myself.

I live in fear but also in bitterness. I'm out here working out and trying and my body consistently flips me the middle finger and does what it wants. In early April 2016, I posted a Blue Apron meal to my blog and shared my disdain that after eating both kale AND plantains, both things I wouldn't typically buy or eat, I still did not look like Jennifer Lawrence.

To me it was a mystery. I knew what I was saying was in jest, but it matters in a couple ways. First, it parallels the struggle that we all have when it comes to eating healthy. Sure, some health food tastes good but fattening and/or sugary food always tastes better, at least in my experience. When we begin eating healthy, it's not always easy to accept certain tastes. Who knew a leafy green would become a hot trend and we'd all be forced to try and choke it down, so we can say we've had it? On the other hand, there is merit in trying new foods. I didn't hate the way I prepared kale that day, but I've hated it every time since then. It's gross.

I think the problem is, I've been on this "journey" since 2009. I'm totally over it. I think when I began this process I thought there would be a finish line. I have tried and failed at many diets in my life that include: Richard Simmons (when I was in high school. As I've mentioned, that only lasted about a week because his parameters were insane), Atkins, Slow Carb, Low Carb, No Carb, All Carbs, and a diet where I pretty much just ate bacon. What has worked for me the most has been tracking points and/or calories because it lets me see what I'm eating during the day. At first, I was all about it. I was very overweight when I started, and I had so much momentum. I was strict in a way I never had been. I wouldn't even take small bites of other people's food because I wouldn't know how to count one bite of macaroni and cheese. It worked. When the flame finally died down, I felt insane. Counting for an OCD person has its pros and cons. I'm tracking what I do every day and when I go over one point or calorie, I lose it. Sometimes, I can do it but when I feel I've screwed it up somehow, I have the most intense self-loathing.

The way I view food and failure is dangerous. My goal in writing this book is to get it all out on the page. The truth is, I know *how* to eat. That is, I know what slims my waistline down and what doesn't. What I haven't quite managed to figure out is how to be OK with who I am in the moment. If I hate myself for eating too many chips and queso at a Mexican place (which I do, at least once or twice a month), and I mean really hate myself, I have this mental setback that causes me to go into a shame spiral. Perhaps before I walked into that Mexican joint I felt fine. When I leave, I feel like I've gained 14 pounds and my round face has gotten rounder. I'll touch my belly or arms with disdain because to me, the stretch marks have grown brighter in the past hour.

Maybe, just maybe, I'm not the only one that feels this way. When I started in 2009 the only books I read or images I saw as inspiration were ones by beautiful, motivated people that had 6 packs. I wanted to be one of them. They were "done" y'all. It turns out those people seem to be a rare specimen, like alien contact or a bald eagle sighting. Oh, and there is no "done."

There are people out there, it seems, that use food only for sustenance, enjoy working out and find the meaning of life in a jog or nutrition shake. I am not in any way knocking that. The thing I've realized is, I'm not ever going to be that person. It's not that I don't think I can. Though, if I'm being honest, I am not sure. It's that I don't want that. You know what would happen if I snapped my fingers and suddenly had the body of a 1970s Jane Fonda? Well, I'd walk around naked for a few weeks just because but unless the snap of the fingers also took away my low self-esteem and love of food, I would put the weight back on within a year or two.

Mentality matters. You know what else matters? You. Yes, I know, it's cheesy. And, yes, I need to take my own advice but what I've learned is that I'm an actual human being and I have been an actual human being at every number I've ever been on the scale. And so are you. It's totally acceptable to want to drop a few pounds but do it with a better mentality than I did.

I'm disgusting. I need to lose weight. There's not a guy in the world that would touch me. I would probably suffocate him. People think about your weight the entire time they are with you.

Meet my train of thought prior to losing weight and then again, every time I "cheated" on my diet, then when I started plateauing and finally when I began gaining weight back.

My obsession with counting worked with the scale but how I felt about myself never really changed. That's the problem. By writing this down and seeking professional help, I hope to get to the root of why I'm so hard on myself and also work toward fixing the problem. Maybe we can do that together.

You are Eggscellent!

Spicy Deviled Eggs

I eat eggs nearly every day! Deviled eggs are a staple for me during the holidays. They are probably in my top five favorite foods. I make them in a classic way with mayo and mustard. I do *not* use pickles *or* pickle relish because I believe that pickles are an abomination. They disgust me. You probably know how to make classic deviled eggs, but I wanted to show you a way to make them a bit snazzier.

Ingredients

- 2 eggs
- 2 tablespoons light mayonnaise (REAL mayonnaise, not any "whipped" salad dressing business)
- 1 tablespoon yellow mustard (you could also use Dijon for additional kick)
- 1 teaspoon Sriracha sauce (give or take depending on your tolerance)
- 1 piece turkey bacon (cooked until crisp/I make turkey bacon in the oven) OR 3 pieces of pre-cooked bacon (usually around 80 calories)
- Sliced green onion for garnish
- Salt, pepper, garlic powder, smoked Paprika to taste

Directions:

Hard boil your eggs, cut them in half, dump the yolks in a bowl and mash them up.

Add salt, pepper, and garlic powder. Mix in the mayo, mustard, and hot sauce.

Use the mixture to fill up the egg white halves.

Top with crumbled bacon and green onions. It's so easy!

Regular deviled eggs are delicious but having them this way makes for a nice change to kick things up a bit.

Let Me Holla at a Frittata

Ingredients:

- 2 eggs
- 1 tablespoon water
- 1 tablespoon skim milk
- 1 green onion, sliced
- ½ cup sliced mushrooms
- 3 pieces of thinly sliced deli meat, chopped (turkey, ham, or roast beef)
- 2 tablespoons reduced fat Feta Cheese
- Handful of fresh spinach (chopped)
- Salt, pepper, garlic powder to taste

Directions:

Pre-heat oven to 350 degrees. Spray an oven safe skillet with non-stick spray (I like butter flavored) and let it go on medium heat.

Crack eggs into a bowl and whisk them together. Add spices, water, milk, mushrooms (you can sauté these first and separately if you prefer cooked to fresh), deli meat, and spinach.

Pour mixture into skillet and let it heat on bottom for roughly 3 minutes.

While mixture is in there, sprinkle feta cheese on top.

Stick the whole skillet into the oven and let it stay in there until the eggs are cooked all the way through.

When it comes out, add more cheese if you'd like but also sprinkle the sliced green onions on top for garnish.

Egg in the Clouds

This is also something I wasn't aware existed until adulthood. I wouldn't know personally because I don't have children, but I feel like this could be something that kids like.

Ingredients:

- 4 eggs
- ½ tablespoon grated Parmesan (the real thing or the green stuff in a can)
- Salt, pepper to taste

Note: You'll need either a hand or stand mixer for this

Directions:

Pre-Heat oven to 375 degrees. You'll want a cookie sheet that's sprayed with non-stick spray or covered with parchment paper.

Grab two bowls: one big, one small. In the big one, crack in the egg whites. You'll want to make sure not to break the yolks.

Stick the yolks in the smaller bowl.

Beat the egg whites until you get stiff peaks. That means, when you lift the beaters out of the bowl, the whites form little peaks in both the bowl and on the beater. As in, they look like hair mousse from the 80s.

Fold in the parmesan and add salt.

Grab a serving spoon and make 4 little blobs of egg whites on your cookie sheet.

Take the same spoon, flip it over and make a little dent in all of them so you can put a yolk there. Carefully add the yolks.

Bake them anywhere from 7-15 minutes, depending on how runny you like your yolks.

When they are done, they are good with toast. You can also garnish with more cheese, crumbled bacon, and green onions.

Baked Eggs with Spinach

Ingredients:

- 1 to 2 cups fresh spinach
- 2 eggs
- 2 to 3 tablespoons reduced fat Feta Cheese
- Non-stick cooking spray
- Salt, pepper, garlic powder to taste

Directions:

Pre-heat oven to 400 degrees. Take a non-stick pan, add the spinach and about a tablespoon of water. Cook it until it cooks down to about half the size.

Take a small casserole dish and spray it with non-stick spray. Lay the spinach out across the bottom of the dish.

Crack two eggs on top of the spinach. Top that with salt, pepper, and garlic powder. Sprinkle the top with cheese.

Depending on how you like your yolks, pop it in the oven from anywhere from 15 minutes until the end of time.

I like a runny yolk, so I check the eggs constantly and they go from raw to overdone in a matter of seconds so just keep an eye on them.

14

Put the Past Behind You

Self-deprecation is kind of my "shtick." I enjoy making people uncomfortable by berating myself. It's one of those defense mechanisms you hear about your whole life. It doesn't take a rocket scientist to figure out that I talk about myself so someone else doesn't do it first. As an adult, I should realize that it's much less likely for someone to hurl fat jokes my way than it was in high school, but I still feel like that girl who lives in paralyzing fear of being humiliated because of my weight.

Now, when I make a comment about my body, I usually get a refutation. For example, if I say, "I'm fat" and someone says, "No you're not. You're beautiful," there's problems all up in that. First of all, why am I saying that? Am I saying it for someone to say I'm not fat? To agree? Am I just being factual? What am I looking for when I say that? Second, when someone says, "You aren't fat. You're beautiful," their intentions are pure. We've been taught to believe that fat is ugly. Therefore, it's our job to tell people they aren't ugly.

When we equate fat with ugly, we perpetuate the problem. I am not so much talking to people who come back with the "you aren't fat, you're beautiful" comments. I'm talking to those of us who consistently rag on ourselves in public or in our own minds. If we believe fat is equal to ugly, it's difficult to ever get out of that mindset.

I go back and read old blog posts and see how sad or scared I've been for years and it's alarming. It seems like I've been telling myself I'm not worthy of love because I've put on weight. Let's stop doing that.

Don't live in fear. Take one day at a time to loosen the iron chains that have burned scars into your wrists and held you down all these years. You owe it to yourself.

Life is a constant shit show of embarrassment. I always manage to equate any small failure to my weight. I remember every fall, every typo I've ever made. The biggest fall(s) I've ever made came at a funeral. It happened over a decade ago and it still haunts me.

As I mentioned earlier, I had foot surgery in college to combat my painfully flat feet. After the surgery, my great grandmother died. I don't mean to speak ill of the dead, but my 96 year old great grandma could not have chosen a worse time to kick the bucket. I had to attend her funeral right after I got a heavy cast and I could barely function on the crutches.

When we arrived at the funeral in Crossville it was December and the mountains of Tennessee never disappoint with wintry weather. There had been snowy storms that week that included all forms of precipitation: rain, snow, sleet, etc. We got out of the car and I propped my crutches on the slick asphalt of the concrete. Immediately the rubber stoppers on the bottom of the crutches started sliding everywhere. It hadn't even been two weeks since I had surgery, so my cast was around 8 pounds and the rest of my weight only made it more difficult. I placed both crutches in front of me and began the trek to the front door. Carpet was a savior in those days, but I had at least 50 feet to go before I could feel safe.

Each step took a deep breath and a considerable amount of pain. I know I'm building this up as if I'm a telling a tale of heroism but it's my story, my book and why not make it look like I had the worst foot surgery and the most horrific time with crutches than anyone else on the face of the planet? It was bad. I'm telling you it was. It also helps to build it up, so the next part seems more justified.

I had made it about half way to the front door when I entered into the "yellow paint zone." My mother was freaking out. She always warned me how slippery yellow paint could be and then she would tell me a story about the time she was pregnant with my brother and fell because of slippery yellow paint in the parking lot of a grocery store. It's true, yellow paint is slick, especially with remnants of winter weather resting on top of it.

Just as my mother was giving me yet another warning about the paint, my right rubber stopper slid about a foot away causing my right leg to collapse underneath me and I completely lost control.

Within half a second, my body was splayed out flat in the parking lot, crutches on either side. My hip burned, my foot hurt but more than anything, I wanted to die from embarrassment. My mother lost it. She gasped and ran over to me. My father and brother were feigning concern but doing a horrible job because they couldn't even begin to mask their laughter. I tried to laugh it off too, but the reality was I didn't even know how I was going to stand up.

It felt like one of those moments when the jaws of life may be needed to rescue me. Somehow my mom, dad and brother managed to get me standing again. At that point, I had fallen so each step I took after that was even more terrifying. My parents stayed on either side of me, giving me about 6 inches of space to my left and right.

About a foot before I reached the curb to step up, the exact same thing happened again. It essentially looked like a replay of the fall that happened less than 3 minutes before that. This time, my Dad and brother were full on hysterical and my mother just looked like she didn't know what to do. I lied there, staring at the sky, feeling like an inferior, fat, useless member of society. It is very much like me to spiral out of control with my thoughts like this. I had never seen a skinny person fall twice at a funeral.

At that moment, the funeral director came out to the parking lot. As I lied on the ground, the old man with curly hair and a dingy, tan suit he's clearly used as his "funeral suit" since the 70s picked up my crutches, looked at me, then at my mother and said, "she's using these wrong." In the past I have described my mother in many ways but when it comes to her children and people mistreating them, she's akin to a lioness protecting her cubs. What I'm saying is she will eat you alive and scare everyone else in the surrounding area literally to death.

We all stood in shock listening to the funeral director shame my crutch skills rather than helping me up off the ground. My mother could only take a couple of minutes of this before she grabbed the crutches from him and explained, with rage, that I needed help, not instruction. Before she was able to get the crutches back, he actually did a demonstration as I was still sprawled out on the ground. I mean, who does that? Honestly, we could have sued. We probably would have lost but I think we may have had a case. My general clumsiness didn't lessen the dangerous yellow paint crutch situation I was in. In theory, I used my crutches the rest of the way to get in, but the reality is, I was basically hoisted into the funeral home for fear of a third fall.

When I finally got into a place with secure flooring, I saw my Grandpa running up to me. It was his mother that had died, and he looked totally taken aback. It wasn't his mother's passing that had him distraught, it was the fact that everyone in the funeral home had heard and was discussing the fact that his granddaughter had taken 2 ungracious tumbles in the parking lot.

My Grandpa has always referred to me as "Girl." Until 2 or 3 years ago when I actually heard him say, "Heather," I didn't think he knew my name. "Girl! You scared me to death. Are you OK?!"

My Grandpa isn't what you would call a talker or someone who shows much in the way of emotion, so this only made my embarrassment worse. "I'm fine, Grandpa. I'm sorry. I'm just not good with my crutches." The word fat ass just repeated as a flashing neon sign in my brain the entire night. The event prompted a pretty decent poem, but it was horrifying and yet another blow to my self-esteem.

Literal falls are bad, but sometimes I take figurative falls as well when it comes to my career. As a writer, I'm bound to have typos. I'm especially bad at typing with fury under my fingertips. I write super-fast and leave, quality, refined text in the dust. I come back to it later, trying to pick up the pieces but I have no patience for editing. I have been called out many times for typos in my blog posts and it always makes my face rush with heat because I'm so embarrassed. Those typos are permanently engrained in my mental vision. They make me even more insecure than I already am and chip away at my confidence as a writer.

There was a time in college when I debated the topic of healthcare on a radio station with another fellow student. I felt that I did a pretty nice job, even though my voice was shaking from nerves. After the conversation, I got in a somewhat heated debate with him and his league of bro-friends on Facebook. I don't remember the exact quote but one of the things I typed was, "I shutter to think..." Yes, I wrote, "I shutter."

This was my senior year in college and it was well before Facebook had an edit or delete feature for their comments. It was there, out in the open, for the whole world to see. I misspelled "shudder" and wrote "shutter," as in, "The house needs two new shutters." Y'all, those guys grabbed on to that spelling, wrapped their hands and feet around it and with a vice grip, wouldn't let go. Every ounce of credibility, every hour of research on the topic I was passionate about was completely erased with two t's.

These mistakes move into the space in my brain like an unwelcome houseguest that reiterates the phrase "You're not good enough" on a constant loop.

What would happen if we forgot every "failure" of the past and freed ourselves to only look forward to the future?

What if we thought we were good enough? Pretty enough? Smart enough? Thin enough?

What if we stopped flinging hateful thoughts and comments at ourselves until we are so beaten down we can't live a full, healthy life?

Over the course of both this book and the years I've spent blogging about weight, I have amassed myself with thousands of insults. Many of them are derivatives of the negative comments others have made toward me over the years. I've adopted those comments as my children and assume responsibility for them. Yes, I'm fat. Yes, that means I'm not worth your time. Yes, my writing is mediocre. Yes, I should give up trying to write a book.

Fuck that person in my brain.

It always horrifies and angers my loved ones when I'm self-deprecating. I'm not sure what I hope to gain by using verbal vitriol to berate myself, but I do it. I have talked about my cankles, side boob, arm fat, cellulite, belly, etc. Many people find this type of talk relatable and funny. Maybe I like a laugh? Maybe I feel that if I call myself out, it softens the blow of knowing that those things are true.

All of us, myself included, need to stop treating ourselves like mean girls and start treating ourselves like we would a best friend.

Let go of the past. It may contribute to who you are right now, but it does not have to define your future. Forget what you consider to be old failures. So, what you fell on a first date (that happened to me). You are also an accomplished human being. So, what you don't have a six-pack and drink powdered protein shakes for breakfast? You had a bagel with cream cheese and that shit was delicious. I hope you enjoyed it.

Life is about balance so let's put one foot in front of the other, stop beating ourselves up and release all of the demons that are consistently floating around in our heads.

When You Need It to Be Fast

Chicken Sausage Hobo Meal

Ingredients:

- 1 six pack of pre-cooked chicken sausage (
- 1 cob of corn
- ½ package button mushrooms
- ½ yellow onion
- 1 zucchini, diced
- 1 teaspoon olive oil
- 1 tablespoon low fat butter spread
- Salt, pepper, and garlic powder to taste

Directions:

Fire up the grill. Cut up the chicken sausage, corn cob, zucchini into similar sized pieces. Toss all the ingredients together.

Take a large sheet of aluminum foil and dump all the ingredients on it.

Lift the foil up on each side, creating a closed in pocket. Stick it on the grill for 20 minutes and that's it!

You can add anything you want to this, even potatoes. If you choose to do other ingredients, that's fine but keep in mind that some take longer than others. Potatoes take a long time to cook. You could microwave them a few minutes and then add them to the packet.

Cheatin' Chicken Fiesta Wrap

Sometimes the frozen section can be a blessing. One of my favorite things to do is to take a low carb wrap and combine grilled chicken with something frozen from the freezer. For instance, you can now find broccoli, cheese and rice mixed together in a steaming bag. Combine that with chicken, salt and pepper and you have a Cheesy, Chicken, Broccoli and Rice Wrap in under 5 minutes. I am a BIG fan of burritos, so I use the following recipe for quick lunches to satisfy my need.

Ingredients

- 1 large low carb or low-cal wrap
- 1 frozen Spanish rice meal (you can find these in TV dinner section of your freezer with only rice)
- 1 grilled chicken breast
- 1 tablespoon salsa
- 2 tablespoons low fat shredded cheese
- 2 tablespoons sliced black olives
- 2 tablespoons chopped onion
- Shredded lettuce
- Optional toppings: avocado, guacamole, sour cream, beans

Directions:

Prepare the grilled chicken if you haven't already.

If you have, put the Spanish rice in the microwave for the required time.

While that's happening, start assembling your burrito by shredding the chicken and adding the rest of the toppings.

When the rice is done, split in half and add to the burrito. Use the second half for your next burrito.

Quick & Easy Chicken Tostadas

Ingredients:

- 2 small, soft, taco-sized corn tortillas
- 1 grilled chicken breast
- Shredded lettuce
- 2 tablespoons salsa
- ¼ cup low fat shredded cheese
- 1 chopped green onion

Directions:

Pre-heat oven to 350 degrees. Pop the tortillas in the oven on an aluminum foil covered baking sheet.

While they are in the oven, cut the grilled chicken into strips. There are also several decent brands out there making pre-made chicken strips. You can use those too.

Once the tortillas start bubbling up and toasting in the oven, they are ready to go. You just want them to get crunchy without having to fry them.

Take them out, top with chicken and the rest of the ingredients.

Spreading a layer of refried beans before adding the chicken and/or topping with low fat sour cream would also be good

.

15

Stop Punishing Yourself
Try Love Instead

Since I have started this journey, I've had tremendous success losing weight, but I've also put a lot back on. From the moment I started losing weight, I began criticizing myself. Even after losing 115 pounds, I couldn't be happy with who I was. Then, when I started gaining it back, it's been a series of self-punishment.

Punishing myself has affected both my mental and physical health and my relationships with others.

There are people out there in the world who aren't evil. They are nice and have no ulterior motives. Why is it then when someone gives me a compliment I want to slap them across the face and tell them to go to hell? I don't think I've ever accepted a compliment without some obnoxious protest.

One of my goals is to accept the fact that I have some success in life due to hard work and luck and that no matter what weight I am, I can clean up pretty well occasionally. I figure if I can convince myself of that, I can be better about accepting compliments from genuine people.

"You look pretty." –Kind friend

"I'm a fat cow." –Me, making it awkward

"Congrats on getting that extra teaching job." –my therapist

"I wouldn't have to take these extra jobs if I wasn't so damn poor." –me, "keeping it real"

"Oh, I like that dress!" –Unsuspecting Stranger

"It barely fits me and cost me like 5 dollars." me, scaring them off

"This macaroni and cheese is delicious, boo." –my boyfriend

"So, you hated the chicken?" me, lottery winner of boyfriends

"I really liked your talk on mental health in female literary characters." –fellow teacher

"Yeah, well, you have a book and I don't so whatever." me, being generally awful

Why am I like this? Why can't I bottle up my self-doubt like everyone else does and fake it? No, I have to make it known that I think I'm under-qualified, overweight, or inadequate. My reactions are not only annoying but also rude. I'm not saying I should sugarcoat my feelings but there's no need in accosting someone just because I have issues with myself.

The point is, learn to accept compliments politely and with confidence that the person on the other end actually means it because more than likely, they do. I'm preaching to myself here. Also, because I'm so outraged by my looks and my position in my professional/creative life sometimes that I am selfish. I don't notice when others succeed. So, because of that, I've really been working on being nice to others and congratulating them when they do something great. Overall, I'm trying to be a better person.

It actually works. I notice imperfections much less now and try to share the love people have given me. The goal is to one day believe the compliments people give me are true because I've decided I'm not so bad after all. I'm getting there slowly but surely.

Having said that, I have to give a PSA for people out there who feel the need to comment on someone's weight loss. In general, it seems that people have no tact when they see someone they know has lost a significant amount of weight. There are certain tactics to avoid.

Before addressing the way people talk to others that have lost weight, I want to make note about the way you treat someone who is on a strict diet. There are people out there who feel like it's necessary to pressure you into eating or drinking food they've prepared or food that they are partaking in.

"You can have just a little bite." The pressure doesn't end there. A lot of times it's excessive. A person on a diet that has will power is in control of their situation and food intake. They aren't being rude. They are being aware of what they are putting in their body.

If you go to someone's house and they have prepared you a meal, understandably, you want to take them up on it, but you don't have to eat everything, and you definitely don't have to have dessert. Simply tell them you're too full. If you are thinking about your pushy friends or family, be as polite as you can but if they don't stop, you have every right to put your foot down. If you are the pushy person: stop. It's annoying.

This next message is for people who work at grocery stores or in the restaurant industry. If I'm in your line and all I have is a pack of Double Stuft Oreos and a pint of Red Velvet Cake Ben & Jerry's Ice Cream, I'm probably not in the mood for you to say, "Someone's hungry."

If I'm at a restaurant with my friend and you are my server, please don't feel the need to point out that your desserts are big enough for two people implying that we should share. I want what I want. I especially hate when a server comes back to the table after I've left nothing and says something like, "I guess you didn't like it" with this sarcastic tone.

There was a time when my best friend Jordan lived with his Great Aunt and we hung out there all the time. We met there every Thursday night to watch *Grey's Anatomy*. Food has always, pardon the pun, been on the table when Jordan and I are together. One night in particular, we had pizza (2), breadsticks and our favorite go-to dessert, Turtle Pie.

His aunt came in, surveyed the kitchen, and announced that once we got done eating "all that" there was a pound cake in the refrigerator. That was several years ago, and Jordan and I still say we are eating "all that" all the time. The point is, we remember when people make comments on what we weigh or what we are eating. Just remember that before you say something.

There are also ways to compliment people who have lost weight. When I began losing weight, it took about 30 pounds before people commented at all. I had someone ask me if I had new perfume or if I got a haircut. People would say, "You look nice today," with an inflection at the end of their voice like they were asking a question.

They made it seem like I just looked a little less sloppy. I got several comments like this and finally I said to someone, "Well, no I don't have new perfume, but I've lost 30 pounds."

They responded, "That's it! Good for you!"

After I lost over 100 pounds, I started getting the whole "You've lost a *ton* of weight," commentary. I know, I know, I sound sensitive. Truth be told, weight is about the only thing that I'm sensitive about (blatant lie) but it just makes sense to me that you wouldn't want to ever use the word "ton" to describe how much weight someone has lost. A ton is 2,000 pounds. Give me a little credit here and just go with, "You look great!" How hard would that be?

A woman I used to work with during my initial weight loss would say, "I can really tell today." I know she was being complimentary, but I wanted to shake her and ask her if I looked like a total fat-ass the day before.

Instead, I just said, "Thanks," with my teeth clenched.

Another friend took a look at my before and after picture online and made a point to tell me that I was unrecognizable in the before picture. "I was shocked," she said. "I thought maybe it was a picture of your grandmother or something." I still don't know how to react to that.

I also wish I had a dollar for every time someone has said, "I had no idea you were that big." How do people like that get by in life without someone punching them in the face?

I know that by writing about my weight loss so publicly, I'm responsible for putting myself out there and have to accept the fact that there are people in this world that have no couth, and I just have to deal with them. I've spent a lifetime hearing that I carry my weight well and having nurses or blood donation workers have a look of disbelief when they see my weight.

It happens when I exercise in public too. I cannot tell you how many times someone has stopped me to tell me how amazing I am for running. A woman I don't know outside my gym the other day saw me jogging to warm up, put her hand up to get my attention and said, "I'm so proud of you."

Out of all the other fit looking women around, she chose me to express pride in a complete stranger. Good intentions? Yes. Offensive? Also, yes. I've been working out as an overweight person for years. So have a lot of other people. I'm not a hero.

I'll be honest. The primary culprits of inappropriate comment making: elderly people, cashiers, servers, the rare breed of people who have never once considered their weight as a problem. Here are some key words to avoid: huge, ton, big, stunned, wow, etc. Hopefully you get the point.

A lot of times our insecurities with weight spill over into other areas in our life. Food is a crutch for the problem that we often use because we straight up don't feel we are good enough...for anything. It's a tough realization to come upon but it's one that I know to be true for myself.

I have a Master's degree in writing and wrote my first auto-biography when I was 12. Yet, when someone asks me what I do, I can't ever say, "writer." At first, I thought it was because I was a teacher and writing doesn't pay the bills. Then I realized that I felt weird calling myself a teacher too even though as I mentioned earlier, I have been teaching since I could talk.

Why do I have such an issue with owning who I am and what I do? I used to think people would think I'm dumb if I said, "I'm a writer." Actually, I still think that. When someone says, "I'm a writer," there's definitely a stigma. The question that follows that statement is always, "What do you write about?"

Can I just interject here and say that *being* a writer kind of sucks? It's hard work with little reward (usually) and if your work has the privilege of being published, it's under a microscope. Sure, your mom is always proud of you but none of your academic peers liked it on Facebook so in your mind, you've failed miserably.

I think because I have the knowledge that there are writers out there with tons of books already and are full of more brilliant material to pour out on the page, it makes me feel a word stronger than the word inadequate that I can't think of because I'M NOT A GOOD WRITER AND I WILL NEVER MAKE IT IN LIFE!

What will make me feel I'm good enough to call myself a "writer?" An ISBN number? A review of my work by a famous writer? Or, will it be when I actually have an income amounting to more than a few hundred bucks a year from spilling my guts on a page?

I'm not sure. Calling myself a teacher isn't easy either. Y'all, my title is instructor, I have had hundreds (probably over a thousand now) of students and yet, calling myself "teacher" seems like a title I'm not worthy to hold. If this is you, if you feel like you aren't worthy of a specific title, or that you aren't contributing to society, stop it. Both of us need to stop what we are doing right now and sing our own praises.

If you go to work each day, no matter what job, or if you keep small human beings alive, or if you've been through hell and back and still wake up every morning to attack the day, you are already winning at life. Own who you are in order to be the best possible version of yourself.

Acknowledging your weaknesses is fine, especially if you're working on them. It's good to be aware. However, knowing and speaking your strengths out loud seems like a much more positive way to live your life. You are a flipping rock star. I don't care what those voices in your (my) head say.

The reason living by this mantra is difficult is because we have a jacked up view of success and failure. Before we can change our attitude, we have to stop viewing slipups, numbers on the scale, and comparisons to others as the end all be all components of our self-image.

If I gain a pound, I feel like I've failed. Screw everything I've ever done in my life, I am a loser because of what a scale tells me. If I can't find the energy to work out one day, my whole journey is pointless and dumb. I knew I could never really keep up with being fit forever.

I get a rejection letter from a journal. Of course, I did. I'm a shit writer. My student gave me a bad eval, I don't deserve to stand at the head of the classroom. One blip on the radar should not and does not impact the overall soundtrack of your life.

We are complex characters and basically, you win some you lose some. Stop defining success by the things you haven't done and start defining it by things you have done. We are all works in progress. As in, this whole journey thing? Yeah, it's never over. That sounds terrible, but it just means you're always changing, trying to be better and that's a positive thing.

You are good enough.

You're Cute! Eat Cute Food!

I love wonton recipes, so I'm closing with those. Enjoy!

Wonton Tacos

Ingredients:

- ¼ pound lean ground beef (this is a single serving so feel free to multiple for more than one person)
- 4 Wonton Wrappers
- 1 small pinch each of the following spices: chili powder, garlic powder, onion powder, smoked Paprika, Cumin, salt, and pepper
- ¼ cup light shredded cheese
- Shredded lettuce and salsa to taste
- Non-stick cooking spray

Directions:

Pre-heat oven to 350 degrees. Get out a muffin pan (regular sized muffins) and spray four of the holes with non-stick cooking spray.

Add a wonton to each, trying to make a cup shape.

While the oven is heating up, grab a skillet and heat up your ground beef. Once all the pink is gone, add the spices.

Pop the muffin tin in the oven and let them wrappers bake for 5 minutes.

When it comes out of the oven, divide the meat, cheese, lettuce, and salsa.

There are plenty of other toppings you can add (olives, jalapeños, sour cream, etc.) so just do your favorite.

Mini Shepherd's Pie

Ingredients:

- ¼ pound lean ground beef (again, this is a single serving so multiply if necessary)
- 4 Wonton Wrappers
- 1 single serving cup of instant mashed potatoes (Turn your head if you don't eat processed foods. This is the easiest way to make this. Feel free to go through the trouble of making mashed potatoes if you want. I'll be done eating by the time you finish.)
- 1 teaspoon Worcestershire sauce
- 1 teaspoon tomato paste
- Salt, pepper, garlic powder to taste
- Optional ingredients: frozen peas and carrots

Directions:

Pre-heat oven to 350 degrees. Get out a muffin pan (regular sized muffins) and spray four of the holes with non-stick cooking spray. Add a wonton to each, trying to make a cup shape.

While the oven is heating up, grab a skillet and heat up your ground beef. Immediately add the Worcestershire sauce, salt, pepper, and garlic powder to the skillet.

Go ahead and pop your instant mashed potatoes in the microwave using the instructions on the container.

Once all the pink in the meat is gone, add the tomato paste. Make sure it's all combined. The mixture will be a little thick and sticky.

Put the muffin pan in the oven and let the wontons bake 3-4 minutes (you can do this while you prepare the other ingredients).

Take the muffin pan out, divide the meat into each one. If you are using vegetables, add those on top of the meat.

Once you've done that, divide the mashed potatoes and add them to all four wontons.

Let them bake for 4-5 minutes, or until the top of the mashed potatoes are brown.

These miniature Shepherd's Pies are deceptively filling and delicious!

Non-Fried Cheese Sticks

I find it strange that I find Arby's cheese sticks to be one of my favorite foods on the planet. It's just fried cheese. But it isn't *just* fried cheese, is it? No, it's hot, juicy cheese that pours out when you bite into a crispy, golden fried crust. What sucks is that I have to limit my cheese stick intake, so I came up with an at-home version that will help you overcome your need for grease.

Ingredients:

- 4 small Wonton Wrappers
- 2 pieces low fat string Mozzarella Cheese
- 2 tablespoons of your favorite marinara sauce
- Non-stick cooking spray

Directions:

Preheat your oven to 400 degrees. Take a baking sheet and cover in aluminum foil and parchment paper.

Cut each string cheese in half horizontally.

Take a small wonton, wet your finger with water and trace it around each edge of the wonton.

Add one of the string cheese halves and roll it up, sealing it with your finger.

Do this with each one, and pop it in the oven for 5 minutes.

Take them out, flip them and put them in again.

Serve with marinara sauce.

Wonton Turnover

Wontons, like ice cream cones, can be filled with anything. Add yogurt or low fat whipped cream with chocolate chips or berries or anything that you want.

Ingredients:

- 4 small Wonton Wrappers
- 4 ounces low fat Cream Cheese
- 4 tablespoons favorite jam or jelly (I love homemade strawberry preserves and they work great in this. You could also use sugar free)

Directions:

Preheat your oven to 400 degrees. Take a baking sheet and cover in aluminum foil and parchment paper.

In the middle of each wonton, smear 1 ounce of low fat cream cheese in the middle and then add one tablespoon of the jam to the top of that.

Wet your hands and moisten each edge of the wonton using your finger.

Fold two sides of the wonton, making them meet in the middle.

Bake for 5-7 minutes.

Acknowledgements

I would first like to thank my father and mother: Greg and Tammy Wyatt. You have always been supportive of all my endeavors. It is impossible to express everything you've done for me in one note at the end of this book. I love you both and I'm so grateful to have you in my life...even if I'm grumpy sometimes and it doesn't feel like it.

To my brother, David Wyatt, you are one of my best friends and even though I didn't give birth to you, one of my proudest accomplishments. I hope you know how much you mean to me. I'm sorry for being sappy. I know it's not really our style.

To Jordan and Cassandra: You two have been by my side through everything and when the thought of not having either of you in my life crosses my mind, I find it difficult to breathe. Jordan, you are the kind of support system everyone needs in their life. Cassandra, you are my permanent partner in crime. You are both stuck with me forever.

Ian: You came into my life in the throes of this journey. Without you, this book doesn't make sense. I wouldn't be the same person. I wouldn't know my worth without you. Thank you for everything. I can't wait to inappropriately fish for you to say nice things about me for the rest of our lives.

I'd like to thank my family and the friends that I consider family: Oma, Grandma, Grandpa, Brenda, Lisa, Arianne, Lauren Smith (and an extra thank you to you for crying when I told you about the book), Alicia, Teri, Allie (though she is no longer with us), Katie, Kellie and Kris and everyone in Chattanooga that shares my last name! And thanks to the families of my friends who have treated me like family: the Greenhaw family, the Pittman family and the "family" at Top Shelf and Coppertop.

Thank you to those that read early versions of the manuscript: Tara Spath, Liz Adams, Pat Peake (editor extraordinaire), and Sara Jenkins.

A giant thanks to Megan Cassidy-Hall at *50/50 Press* for believing in me!

A big thank you to trainer Terry Wiggins at 9 Round in Tuscaloosa for kicking my butt and for once saying, "There's *nothing* wrong with you," when I was complaining about my body.

Thanks to all the students, alums, and faculty of the Spalding University MFA Low Residency Program.

To those colleagues who consistently support me: Ashley McWaters, Jason McCall & Rosemary Royston…Thank you.

And thanks to those friends who share a general love of food, beer and laughs that I have enjoyed being around and that have been supporters of the blog from the beginning: Elliott Roberts (extra thanks for the website help), Tyler Crawford (you have no idea how much I appreciate the yearly Chex Mix), Nish Phillips, Jodi Small & Carina Sanchez.

Thank you to my dogs, Major & June, the University of Alabama football team, my childhood friends, Brandie & Monica, Shirley Cate Heine from the Leaf, the English Department at UA, and Drew Rhodes.

I appreciate all of you more than you will ever know.

About the Author

Heather Wyatt is a teacher and writer by day, and food TV junkie by night.

Heather lives in Tuscaloosa, Alabama and has a slight obsession with her two dogs.

She both graduated from and instructs English at the University of Alabama. She received her MFA in poetry from Spalding University in Louisville, Kentucky.

Several of Heather's poems have been featured in a number of journals including *Number One, Puff Puff Prose Poetry and a Play, The Binnacle, ETA, Writers Tribe Review* and many others.

Inspired by her popular blog of the same name, *My Life Without Ranch* is Heather's first book.

You can visit Heather at www.mylifewithoutranch.com/

Or read more about Heather and her work at www.5050press.com